SUSE Linux Enterprise Server 12 - Storage Administration Guide

A catalogue record for this book is available from the Hong Kong Public Libraries.

Published in Hong Kong by Samurai Media Limited.

Email: info@samuraimedia.org

ISBN 978-988-8406-52-4

Contents

Storage Administration Guide

About This Guide

This guide provides information about how to manage storage devices on SUSE Linux Enterprise Server 12 SP1. For information about partitioning and managing devices, see *Book "Deployment Guide", Chapter 14 "Advanced Disk Setup"*. This guide is intended for system administrators.

Many chapters in this manual contain links to additional documentation resources. This includes additional documentation that is available on the system and documentation available on the Internet.

For an overview of the documentation available for your product and the latest documentation updates, refer to http://www.suse.com/doc.

1 Available Documentation

We provide HTML and PDF versions of our books in different languages. The following manuals for users and administrators are available for this product:

Article "Installation Quick Start"

Lists the system requirements and guides you step-by-step through the installation of SUSE Linux Enterprise Server from DVD, or from an ISO image.

Book "Deployment Guide"

Shows how to install single or multiple systems and how to exploit the product inherent capabilities for a deployment infrastructure. Choose from various approaches, ranging from a local installation or a network installation server to a mass deployment using a remote-controlled, highly-customized, and automated installation technique.

Book "Administration Guide"

Covers system administration tasks like maintaining, monitoring and customizing an initially installed system.

Book "Virtualization Guide"

Describes virtualization technology in general, and introduces libvirt—the unified interface to virtualization—and detailed information on specific hypervisors.

Storage Administration Guide

Provides information about how to manage storage devices on a SUSE Linux Enterprise Server.

Book "AutoYaST"

AutoYaST is a system for installing one or more SUSE Linux Enterprise systems automatically and without user intervention, using an AutoYaST profile that contains installation and configuration data. The manual guides you through the basic steps of auto-installation: preparation, installation, and configuration.

Book "Security Guide"

Introduces basic concepts of system security, covering both local and network security aspects. Shows how to use the product inherent security software like AppArmor or the auditing system that reliably collects information about any security-relevant events.

Book "Security and Hardening Guide"

Deals with the particulars of installing and setting up a secure SUSE Linux Enterprise Server, and additional post-installation processes required to further secure and harden that installation. Supports the administrator with security-related choices and decisions.

Book "System Analysis and Tuning Guide"

An administrator's guide for problem detection, resolution and optimization. Find how to inspect and optimize your system by means of monitoring tools and how to efficiently manage resources. Also contains an overview of common problems and solutions and of additional help and documentation resources.

Book "GNOME User Guide"

Introduces the GNOME desktop of SUSE Linux Enterprise Server. It guides you through using and configuring the desktop and helps you perform key tasks. It is intended mainly for end users who want to make efficient use of GNOME as their default desktop.

Find HTML versions of most product manuals in your installed system under `/usr/share/doc/manual` or in the help centers of your desktop. Find the latest documentation updates at http://www.suse.com/doc where you can download PDF or HTML versions of the manuals for your product.

2 Feedback

Several feedback channels are available:

Bugs and Enhancement Requests

For services and support options available for your product, refer to http://www.suse.com/support/.

To report bugs for a product component, go to https://scc.suse.com/support/requests, log in, and click *Create New*.

User Comments

We want to hear your comments about and suggestions for this manual and the other documentation included with this product. Use the User Comments feature at the bottom of each page in the online documentation or go to http://www.suse.com/doc/feedback.html and enter your comments there.

Mail

For feedback on the documentation of this product, you can also send a mail to `doc-team@suse.de`. Make sure to include the document title, the product version and the publication date of the documentation. To report errors or suggest enhancements, provide a concise description of the problem and refer to the respective section number and page (or URL).

3 Documentation Conventions

The following typographical conventions are used in this manual:

- `/etc/passwd`: directory names and file names

- *placeholder*: replace *placeholder* with the actual value

- `PATH`: the environment variable PATH

- `ls`, `--help`: commands, options, and parameters

- `user`: users or groups

- `Alt`, `Alt`–`F1`: a key to press or a key combination; keys are shown in uppercase as on a keyboard

- *File, File › Save As*: menu items, buttons

- `x86_64` This paragraph is only relevant for the x86_64 architecture. The arrows mark the beginning and the end of the text block.
  `System z, POWER` This paragraph is only relevant for the architectures `z Systems` and `POWER`. The arrows mark the beginning and the end of the text block.

- *Dancing Penguins* (Chapter *Penguins*, ↑Another Manual): This is a reference to a chapter in another manual.

I File Systems and Mounting

1 Overview of File Systems in Linux

SUSE Linux Enterprise Server ships with several different file systems from which to choose, including Btrfs, Ext4, Ext3, Ext2, ReiserFS and XFS. Each file system has its own advantages and disadvantages. For a side-by-side feature comparison of the major operating systems in SUSE Linux Enterprise Server, see http://www.suse.com/products/server/technical-information/#FileSystem (File System Support and Sizes).

Professional high-performance setups might require a highly available storage systems. To meet the requirements of high-performance clustering scenarios, SUSE Linux Enterprise Server includes OCFS2 (Oracle Cluster File System 2) and the Distributed Replicated Block Device (DRBD) in the High Availability Extension add-on. These advanced storage systems are not covered in this guide. For information, see the *SUSE Linux Enterprise High Availability Extension Administration Guide* at http://www.suse.com/doc.

With SUSE Linux Enterprise 12, Btrfs is the default file system for the operating system and XFS is the default for all other use cases. SUSE also continues to support the Ext family of file systems, ReiserFS and OCFS2. By default, the Btrfs file system will be set up with subvolumes. Snapshots will be automatically enabled for the root file system using the snapper infrastructure. For more information about snapper, refer to *Book "Administration Guide", Chapter 3 "System Recovery and Snapshot Management with Snapper"*.

1.1 Terminology

metadata

A data structure that is internal to the file system. It ensures that all of the on-disk data is properly organized and accessible. Essentially, it is "data about the data." Almost every file system has its own structure of metadata, which is one reason the file systems show different performance characteristics. It is extremely important to maintain metadata intact, because otherwise all data on the file system could become inaccessible.

inode

A data structure on a file system that contains a variety of information about a file, including size, number of links, pointers to the disk blocks where the file contents are actually stored, and date and time of creation, modification, and access.

journal

In the context of a file system, a journal is an on-disk structure containing a type of log in which the file system stores what it is about to change in the file system's metadata. Journaling greatly reduces the recovery time of a file system because it has no need for the lengthy search process that checks the entire file system at system start-up. Instead, only the journal is replayed.

1.2 Major File Systems in Linux

SUSE Linux Enterprise Server offers a variety of file systems from which to choose. This section contains an overview of how these file systems work and which advantages they offer.

It is very important to remember that no file system best suits all kinds of applications. Each file system has its particular strengths and weaknesses, which must be taken into account. In addition, even the most sophisticated file system cannot replace a reasonable backup strategy.

The terms *data integrity* and *data consistency*, when used in this section, do not refer to the consistency of the user space data (the data your application writes to its files). Whether this data is consistent must be controlled by the application itself.

 Note: Default File Systems on SUSE Linux Enterprise Server 12 SP1

SUSE Linux Enterprise Server 12 SP1 is set up using Btrfs and snapshot support for the root partition by default. See *Book "Administration Guide", Chapter 3 "System Recovery and Snapshot Management with Snapper"* for details. Data partitions (such as /home residing on a separate partition) are formatted with XFS by default.

Important: The YaST Partitioner

Unless stated otherwise in this section, all the steps required to set up or change partitions and file systems can be performed by using the YaST Partitioner (which is also strongly recommended). For information, see *Book "Deployment Guide", Chapter 14 "Advanced Disk Setup"*.

1.2.1   Btrfs

Btrfs is a copy-on-write (COW) file system developed by Chris Mason. It is based on COW-friendly B-trees developed by Ohad Rodeh. Btrfs is a logging-style file system. Instead of journaling the block changes, it writes them in a new location, then links the change in. Until the last write, the new changes are not committed.

1.2.1.1   Key Features

Btrfs provides fault tolerance, repair, and easy management features, such as the following:

- Writable snapshots that allow you to easily roll back your system if needed after applying updates, or to back up files.

- Subvolume support: Btrfs creates a default subvolume in its assigned pool of space. It allows you to create additional subvolumes that act as individual file systems within the same pool of space. The number of subvolumes is limited only by the space allocated to the pool.

- The online check and repair functionality `scrub` is available as part of the Btrfs command line tools. It verifies the integrity of data and metadata, assuming the tree structure is fine. You can run scrub periodically on a mounted file system; it runs as a background process during normal operation.

- Different RAID levels for metadata and user data.

- Different checksums for metadata and user data to improve error detection.

- Integration with Linux Logical Volume Manager (LVM) storage objects.

- Integration with the YaST Partitioner and AutoYaST on SUSE Linux Enterprise Server. This also includes creating a Btrfs file system on Multiple Devices (MD) and Device Mapper (DM) storage configurations.

- Offline migration from existing Ext2, Ext3, and Ext4 file systems.

- Boot loader support for `/boot`, allowing to boot from a Btrfs partition.

- Multivolume Btrfs is supported in RAID0, RAID1, and RAID10 profiles in SUSE Linux Enterprise Server 12 SP1. Higher RAID levels are not supported yet, but might be enabled with a future service pack.

- Use Btrfs commands to set up transparent compression.

1.2.1.2 The Root File System Setup on SUSE Linux Enterprise Server

By default, SUSE Linux Enterprise Server is set up using Btrfs and snapshots for the root partition. Snapshots allow you to easily roll back your system if needed after applying updates, or to back up files. Snapshots can easily be managed with the SUSE Snapper infrastructure as explained in *Book "Administration Guide", Chapter 3 "System Recovery and Snapshot Management with Snapper"*. For general information about the SUSE Snapper project, see the Snapper Portal wiki at OpenSUSE.org (http://snapper.io).

When using a snapshot to roll back the system, it must be ensured that data such as user's home directories, Web and FTP server contents or log files do not get lost or overwritten during a roll back. This is achieved by using Btrfs subvolumes on the root file system. Subvolumes can be excluded from snapshots. The default root file system setup on SUSE Linux Enterprise Server as proposed by YaST during the installation contains the following subvolumes. They are excluded from snapshots for the reasons given below.

DEFAULT SUBVOLUME SETUP FOR THE ROOT PARTITION

`/boot/grub2/i386-pc`, `/boot/grub2/x86_64-efi`, `/boot/grub2/powerpc-ieee1275`, `/boot/grub2/s390x-emu`

> A rollback of the boot loader configuration is not supported. The directories listed above are architecture-specific. The first two directories are present on x86_64 machines, the latter two on IBM POWER and on IBM z Systems, respectively.

`/home`

> If `/home` does not reside on a separate partition, it is excluded to avoid data loss on rollbacks.

`/opt`, `/var/opt`

> Third-party products and add-ons usually get installed to `/opt`. It is excluded to avoid uninstalling these applications on rollbacks.

`/srv`

> Contains data for Web and FTP servers. It is excluded to avoid data loss on rollbacks.

`/tmp`, `/var/tmp`, `/var/crash`

> All directories containing temporary files are excluded from snapshots.

`/usr/local`

> This directory is used when manually installing software. It is excluded to avoid uninstalling these installations on rollbacks.

`/var/lib/libvirt/images`

Default directory for all VM images created via libvirt. Excluded from snapshots. By default, this subvolume is created with the option `no copy on write`.

`/var/lib/named`

Contains zone data for the DNS server. Excluded from snapshots to ensure a name server can operate after a rollback.

`/var/lib/mailman`, `/var/spool`

Directories containing mail queues or mail are excluded to avoid a loss of mail after a rollback.

`/var/lib/mariadb`

For the MariaDB data. Excluded from snapshots. By default, this subvolume is created with the option `no copy on write`.

`/var/lib/pgsql`

Contains PostgreSQL data. Excluded from snapshots. By default, this subvolume is created with the option `no copy on write`.

`/var/log`

Log file location. Excluded from snapshots to allow log file analysis after the rollback of a broken system.

 ## Warning: Support for Rollbacks

Rollbacks are only supported by the SUSE support if you do not remove any of the preconfigured subvolumes. You may, however, add additional subvolumes using the YaST Partitioner.

1.2.1.2.1   Mounting Compressed Btrfs File Systems

Note: GRUB 2 and LZO Compressed Root

GRUB 2 cannot read an lzo compressed root. You need a separate `/boot` partition if you want to use compression.

Since SLE12 SP1, compression for Btrfs file systems is supported. Use the `compress` or `compress-force` option and select the compression algorithm, `lzo` or `zlib` (the default). The zlib compression has a higher compression ratio while lzo is faster and takes less CPU load.

For example:

```
root # mount -o compress /dev/sdx /mnt
```

In case you create a file, write to it, and the compressed result is greater or equal to the uncompressed size, Btrfs will skip compression for future write operations forever for this file. If you do not like this behavior, use the `compress-force` option. This can be useful for files that have some initial uncompressible data.

Note, compression takes effect for new files only. Files that were written without compression are not compressed when the file system is mounted with the `compress` or `compress-force` option. Furthermore, files with the `nodatacow` attribute never get their extents compressed:

```
root # chattr +C FILE
root # mount -o nodatacow /dev/sdx /mnt
```

In regard to encryption, this is independent from any compression. After you have written some data to this partition, print the details:

```
root # btrfs filesystem show /mnt
btrfs filesystem show /mnt
Label: 'Test-Btrfs'  uuid: 62f0c378-e93e-4aa1-9532-93c6b780749d
        Total devices 1 FS bytes used 3.22MiB
      devid    1 size 2.00GiB used 240.62MiB path /dev/sdb1
```

If you want this to be permanent, add the `compress` or `compress-force` option into the `/etc/fstab` configuration file. For example:

```
UUID=1a2b3c4d /home btrfs subvol=@/home,compress 0 0
```

A system rollback from a snapshot on SUSE Linux Enterprise Server is performed by booting from the snapshot first. This allows you to check the snapshot while running before doing the rollback. Being able to boot from snapshots is achieved by mounting the subvolumes (which would normally not be necessary).

In addition to the subvolumes listed at *Default Subvolume Setup for the Root Partition* a volume named @ exists. This is the default subvolume that will be mounted as the root partition (/). The other subvolumes will be mounted into this volume.

When booting from a snapshot, not the @ subvolume will be used, but rather the snapshot. The parts of the file system included in the snapshot will be mounted read-only as /. The other subvolumes will be mounted writable into the snapshot. This state is temporary by default: the previous configuration will be restored with the next reboot. To make it permanent, execute the **snapper rollback** command. This will make the snapshot that is currently booted the new *default* subvolume, which will be used after a reboot.

1.2.1.3   Migration from Ext and ReiserFS File Systems to Btrfs

You can migrate data volumes from existing Ext (Ext2, Ext3, or Ext4) or ReiserFS to the Btrfs file system. The conversion process occurs offline and in place on the device. The file system needs at least 15% of available free space on the device.

To convert the file system to Btrfs, take the file system offline, then enter:

```
sudo btrfs-convert <device>
```

To roll back the migration to the original file system, take the file system offline, then enter:

```
sudo btrfs-convert -r <device>
```

 Important: Possible Loss of Data

> When rolling back to the original file system, all data will be lost that you added after the conversion to Btrfs. That is, only the original data is converted back to the previous file system.

1.2.1.4   Btrfs Administration

Btrfs is integrated in the YaST Partitioner and AutoYaST. It is available during the installation to allow you to set up a solution for the root file system. You can use the YaST Partitioner after the installation to view and manage Btrfs volumes.

Btrfs administration tools are provided in the `btrfsprogs` package. For information about using Btrfs commands, see the **man 8 btrfs**, **man 8 btrfsck**, and **man 8 mkfs.btrfs** commands. For information about Btrfs features, see the *Btrfs wiki* at http://btrfs.wiki.kernel.org.

1.2.1.5   Btrfs Quota Support for Subvolumes

The Btrfs root file system subvolumes `/var/log`, `/var/crash` and `/var/cache` can use all of the available disk space during normal operation, and cause a system malfunction. To help avoid this situation, SUSE Linux Enterprise Server now offers Btrfs quota support for subvolumes. If you set up the root file system by using the respective YaST proposal, it is prepared accordingly: quota groups (`qgroup`) for all subvolumes are already set up. To set a quota for a subvolume in the root file system, proceed as follows:

1. Enable quota support:

   ```
   sudo btrfs quota enable /
   ```

2. Get a list of subvolumes:

   ```
   sudo btrfs subvolume list /
   ```

   Quotas can only be set for existing subvolumes.

3. Set a quota for one of the subvolumes that was listed in the previous step. A subvolume can either be identified by path (for example `/var/tmp`) or by `0/subvolume id` (for example `0/272`). The following example sets a quota of five GB for `/var/tmp`.

   ```
   sudo btrfs qgroup limit 5G /var/tmp
   ```

   The size can either be specified in bytes (5000000000), kilobytes (5000000K), megabytes (5000M), or gigabytes (5G). The resulting values in bytes slightly differ, since 1024 Bytes = 1 KiB, 1024 KiB = 1 MiB, etc.

4. To list the existing quotas, use the following command. The column `max_rfer` shows the quota in bytes.

```
sudo btrfs qgroup show -r /
```

 Tip: Nullifying a Quota

In case you want to nullify an existing quota, set a quota size of `0`:

```
sudo btrfs qgroup limit 0 /var/tmp
```

To disable quota support for a partition and all its subvolumes, use **btrfs quota disable**:

```
sudo btrfs quota disable /
```

See the **man 8 btrfs-qgroup** and **man 8 btrfs-quota** for more details. The *UseCases* page on the Btrfs wiki (https://btrfs.wiki.kernel.org/index.php/UseCases) also provides more information.

1.2.1.6 Data Deduplication Support

Btrfs supports data deduplication by replacing identical blocks in the file system with logical links to a single copy of the block in a common storage location. SUSE Linux Enterprise Server provides the tool **duperemove** for scanning the file system for identical blocks. When used on a Btrfs file system, it can also be used to deduplicate these blocks. duperemove is not installed by default. To make it available, install the package `duperemove`.

 Note: Use Cases

As of SUSE Linux Enterprise Server 12 SP1 duperemove is not suited to deduplicate the entire file system. It is intended to be used to deduplicate a set of 10 to 50 large files that possibly have lots of blocks in common, such as virtual machine images.

duperemove can either operate on a list of files or recursively scan a directory:

```
sudo duperemove [options] file1 file2 file3
```

```
sudo duperemove -r [options] directory
```

It operates in two modes: read-only and de-duping. When run in read-only mode (that is without the -d switch), it scans the given files or directories for duplicated blocks and prints them out. This works on any file system.

Running **duperemove** in de-duping mode is only supported on Btrfs file systems. After having scanned the given files or directories, the duplicated blocks will be submitted for deduplication.

For more information see **man 8 duperemove**.

1.2.2   XFS

Originally intended as the file system for their IRIX OS, SGI started XFS development in the early 1990s. The idea behind XFS was to create a high-performance 64-bit journaling file system to meet extreme computing challenges. XFS is very good at manipulating large files and performs well on high-end hardware. XFS is the default file system for data partitions in SUSE Linux Enterprise Server.

A quick review of XFS's key features explains why it might prove to be a strong competitor for other journaling file systems in high-end computing.

1.2.2.1   High Scalability by Using Allocation Groups

At the creation time of an XFS file system, the block device underlying the file system is divided into eight or more linear regions of equal size. Those are called *allocation groups*. Each allocation group manages its own inodes and free disk space. Practically, allocation groups can be seen as file systems in a file system. Because allocation groups are rather independent of each other, more than one of them can be addressed by the kernel simultaneously. This feature is the key to XFS's great scalability. Naturally, the concept of independent allocation groups suits the needs of multiprocessor systems.

1.2.2.2   High Performance through Efficient Management of Disk Space

Free space and inodes are handled by B^+ trees inside the allocation groups. The use of B^+ trees greatly contributes to XFS's performance and scalability. XFS uses *delayed allocation*, which handles allocation by breaking the process into two pieces. A pending transaction is stored in

RAM and the appropriate amount of space is reserved. XFS still does not decide where exactly (in file system blocks) the data should be stored. This decision is delayed until the last possible moment. Some short-lived temporary data might never make its way to disk, because it is obsolete by the time XFS decides where actually to save it. In this way, XFS increases write performance and reduces file system fragmentation. Because delayed allocation results in less frequent write events than in other file systems, it is likely that data loss after a crash during a write is more severe.

1.2.2.3   Preallocation to Avoid File System Fragmentation

Before writing the data to the file system, XFS *reserves* (preallocates) the free space needed for a file. Thus, file system fragmentation is greatly reduced. Performance is increased because the contents of a file are not distributed all over the file system.

 Note: The new XFS On-disk Format

Starting with version 12, SUSE Linux Enterprise Server supports the new "on-disk format" (v5) of the XFS file system. XFS file systems created by YaST will use this new format. The main advantages of this format are automatic checksums of all XFS metadata, file type support, and support for a larger number of access control lists for a file.

Note that this format is *not* supported by SUSE Linux Enterprise kernels older than version 3.12, by xfsprogs older than version 3.2.0, and GRUB 2 versions released before SUSE Linux Enterprise 12. This will be problematic if the file system should also be used from systems not meeting these prerequisites.

If you require interoperability of the XFS file system with older SUSE systems or other Linux distributions, format the file system manually using the `mkfs.xfs` command. This will create an XFS file system in the old format (unless you use the `-m crc=1` option).

1.2.3   Ext2

The origins of Ext2 go back to the early days of Linux history. Its predecessor, the Extended File System, was implemented in April 1992 and integrated in Linux 0.96c. The Extended File System underwent a number of modifications and, as Ext2, became the most popular Linux file system for years. With the creation of journaling file systems and their short recovery times, Ext2 became less important.

A brief summary of Ext2's strengths might help understand why it was—and in some areas still is—the favorite Linux file system of many Linux users.

1.2.3.1   Solidity and Speed

Being quite an "old-timer," Ext2 underwent many improvements and was heavily tested. This might be the reason people often refer to it as rock-solid. After a system outage when the file system could not be cleanly unmounted, e2fsck starts to analyze the file system data. Metadata is brought into a consistent state and pending files or data blocks are written to a designated directory (called `lost+found`). In contrast to journaling file systems, e2fsck analyzes the entire file system and not only the recently modified bits of metadata. This takes significantly longer than checking the log data of a journaling file system. Depending on file system size, this procedure can take half an hour or more. Therefore, it is not desirable to choose Ext2 for any server that needs high availability. However, because Ext2 does not maintain a journal and uses significantly less memory, it is sometimes faster than other file systems.

1.2.3.2   Easy Upgradability

Because Ext3 is based on the Ext2 code and shares its on-disk format and its metadata format, upgrades from Ext2 to Ext3 are very easy.

1.2.4   Ext3

Ext3 was designed by Stephen Tweedie. Unlike all other next-generation file systems, Ext3 does not follow a completely new design principle. It is based on Ext2. These two file systems are very closely related to each other. An Ext3 file system can be easily built on top of an Ext2 file system. The most important difference between Ext2 and Ext3 is that Ext3 supports journaling. In summary, Ext3 has three major advantages to offer:

1.2.4.1   Easy and Highly Reliable Upgrades from Ext2

The code for Ext2 is the strong foundation on which Ext3 could become a highly acclaimed next-generation file system. Its reliability and solidity are elegantly combined in Ext3 with the advantages of a journaling file system. Unlike transitions to other journaling file systems, such as ReiserFS or XFS, which can be quite tedious (making backups of the entire file system and re-creating it from scratch), a transition to Ext3 is a matter of minutes. It is also very safe, because re-creating an entire file system from scratch might not work flawlessly. Considering the number of existing Ext2 systems that await an upgrade to a journaling file system, you can easily see why Ext3 might be of some importance to many system administrators. Downgrading from Ext3 to Ext2 is as easy as the upgrade. Perform a clean unmount of the Ext3 file system and remount it as an Ext2 file system.

1.2.4.2   Reliability and Performance

Some other journaling file systems follow the "metadata-only" journaling approach. This means your metadata is always kept in a consistent state, but this cannot be automatically guaranteed for the file system data itself. Ext3 is designed to take care of both metadata and data. The degree of "care" can be customized. Enabling Ext3 in the `data=journal` mode offers maximum security (data integrity), but can slow down the system because both metadata and data are journaled. A relatively new approach is to use the `data=ordered` mode, which ensures both data and metadata integrity, but uses journaling only for metadata. The file system driver collects all data blocks that correspond to one metadata update. These data blocks are written to disk before the metadata is updated. As a result, consistency is achieved for metadata and data without sacrificing performance. A third option to use is `data=writeback`, which allows data to be written to the main file system after its metadata has been committed to the journal. This option is often considered the best in performance. It can, however, allow old data to reappear in files after crash and recovery while internal file system integrity is maintained. Ext3 uses the `data=ordered` option as the default.

1.2.4.3   Converting an Ext2 File System into Ext3

To convert an Ext2 file system to Ext3:

1. Create an Ext3 journal by running **tune2fs -j** as the `root` user.
   This creates an Ext3 journal with the default parameters.
   To specify how large the journal should be and on which device it should reside, run **tune2fs** -J instead together with the desired journal options `size=` and `device=`. More information about the **tune2fs** program is available in the **tune2fs** man page.

2. Edit the file `/etc/fstab` as the `root` user to change the file system type specified for the corresponding partition from `ext2` to `ext3`, then save the changes.

This ensures that the Ext3 file system is recognized as such. The change takes effect after the next reboot.

3. To boot a root file system that is set up as an Ext3 partition, add the modules `ext3` and `jbd` in the `initrd`. Do so by

   a. adding the following line to `/etc/dracut.conf.d/01-dist.conf`:

   ```
   force_drivers+="ext3 jbd"
   ```

   b. and running the **dracut** -f command.

4. Reboot the system.

1.2.4.4 Ext3 File System Inode Size and Number of Inodes

An inode stores information about the file and its block location in the file system. To allow space in the inode for extended attributes and ACLs, the default inode size for Ext3 was increased from 128 bytes on SLES 10 to 256 bytes on SLES 11. As compared to SLES 10, when you make a new Ext3 file system on SLES 11, the default amount of space preallocated for the same number of inodes is doubled, and the usable space for files in the file system is reduced by that amount. Thus, you must use larger partitions to accommodate the same number of inodes and files than were possible for an Ext3 file system on SLES 10.

When you create a new Ext3 file system, the space in the inode table is preallocated for the total number of inodes that can be created. The bytes-per-inode ratio and the size of the file system determine how many inodes are possible. When the file system is made, an inode is created for every bytes-per-inode bytes of space:

```
number of inodes = total size of the file system divided by the number of bytes per
  inode
```

The number of inodes controls the number of files you can have in the file system: one inode for each file. To address the increased inode size and reduced usable space available, the default for the bytes-per-inode ratio was increased from 8192 bytes on SLES 10 to 16384 bytes on SLES 11. The doubled ratio means that the number of files that can be created is one-half of the number of files possible for an Ext3 file system on SLES 10.

Important: Changing the Inode Size of an Existing Ext3 File System

After the inodes are allocated, you cannot change the settings for the inode size or bytes-per-inode ratio. No new inodes are possible without re-creating the file system with different settings, or unless the file system gets extended. When you exceed the maximum number of inodes, no new files can be created on the file system until some files are deleted.

When you make a new Ext3 file system, you can specify the inode size and bytes-per-inode ratio to control inode space usage and the number of files possible on the file system. If the blocks size, inode size, and bytes-per-inode ratio values are not specified, the default values in the `/etc/mked2fs.conf` file are applied. For information, see the `mke2fs.conf(5)` man page.

Use the following guidelines:

- **Inode size:** The default inode size is 256 bytes. Specify a value in bytes that is a power of 2 and equal to 128 or larger in bytes and up to the block size, such as 128, 256, 512, and so on. Use 128 bytes only if you do not use extended attributes or ACLs on your Ext3 file systems.

- **Bytes-per-inode ratio:** The default bytes-per-inode ratio is 16384 bytes. Valid bytes-per-inode ratio values must be a power of 2 equal to 1024 or greater in bytes, such as 1024, 2048, 4096, 8192, 16384, 32768, and so on. This value should not be smaller than the block size of the file system, because the block size is the smallest chunk of space used to store data. The default block size for the Ext3 file system is 4 KB.

  In addition, you should consider the number of files and the size of files you need to store. For example, if your file system will have many small files, you can specify a smaller bytes-per-inode ratio, which increases the number of inodes. If your file system will have very large files, you can specify a larger bytes-per-inode ratio, which reduces the number of possible inodes.

  Generally, it is better to have too many inodes than to run out of them. If you have too few inodes and very small files, you could reach the maximum number of files on a disk that is practically empty. If you have too many inodes and very large files, you might have free space reported but be unable to use it because you cannot create new files in space reserved for inodes.

If you do not use extended attributes or ACLs on your Ext3 file systems, you can restore the SLES 10 behavior specifying 128 bytes as the inode size and 8192 bytes as the bytes-per-inode ratio when you make the file system. Use any of the following methods to set the inode size and bytes-per-inode ratio:

- **Modifying the default settings for all new Ext3 files:** In a text editor, modify the defaults section of the /etc/mke2fs.conf file to set the inode_size and inode_ratio to the desired default values. The values apply to all new Ext3 file systems. For example:

```
blocksize = 4096
inode_size = 128
inode_ratio = 8192
```

- **At the command line:** Pass the inode size (-I 128) and the bytes-per-inode ratio (-i 8192) to the **mkfs.ext3(8)** command or the **mke2fs(8)** command when you create a new Ext3 file system. For example, use either of the following commands:

```
sudo mkfs.ext3 -b 4096 -i 8092 -I 128 /dev/sda2
sudo mke2fs -t ext3 -b 4096 -i 8192 -I 128 /dev/sda2
```

- **During installation with YaST:** Pass the inode size and bytes-per-inode ratio values when you create a new Ext3 file system during the installation. In the YaST Partitioner on the *Edit Partition* page under *Formatting Options*, select *Format partitionExt3*, then click *Options*. In the *File system options* dialog, select the desired values from the *Block Size in Bytes, Bytes-per-inode,* and *Inode Size* drop-down box.

For example, select 4096 for the *Block Size in Bytes* drop-down box, select 8192 from the *Bytes per inode* drop-down box, select 128 from the *Inode Size* drop-down box, then click *OK*.

File system options:

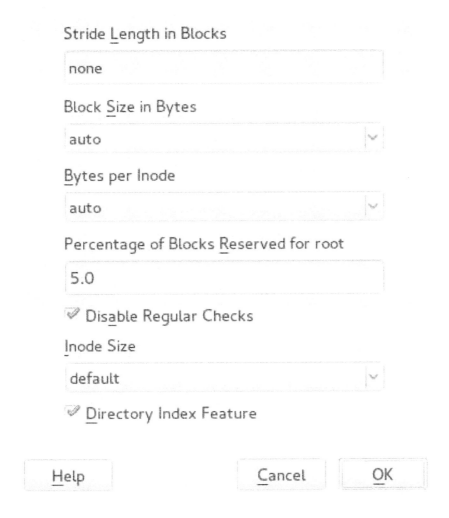

Stride **L**ength in Blocks

```
none
```

Block **S**ize in Bytes

```
auto
```

Bytes per Inode

```
auto
```

Percentage of Blocks **R**eserved for root

```
5.0
```

☑ Dis**a**ble Regular Checks

Inode Size

```
default
```

☑ **D**irectory Index Feature

Help		**C**ancel	**OK**

- **During installation with AutoYaST:** In an AutoYaST profile, you can use the
  fs_options tag to set the opt_bytes_per_inode ratio value of 8192 for -i and the
  opt_inode_density value of 128 for -I:

```
<partitioning config:type="list">
  <drive>
    <device>/dev/sda</device>
    <initialize config:type="boolean">true</initialize>
```

```
<partitions config:type="list">
  <partition>
    <filesystem config:type="symbol">ext3</filesystem>
    <format config:type="boolean">true</format>
    <fs_options>
      <opt_bytes_per_inode>
        <option_str>-i</option_str>
        <option_value>8192</option_value>
      </opt_bytes_per_inode>
      <opt_inode_density>
        <option_str>-I</option_str>
        <option_value>128</option_value>
      </opt_inode_density>
    </fs_options>
    <mount>/</mount>
    <partition_id config:type="integer">131</partition_id>
    <partition_type>primary</partition_type>
    <size>25G</size>
  </partition>
</partitions>
</drive>
<partitioning>
```

For information, see http://www.suse.com/support/kb/doc.php?id=7009075 (*SLES11 ext3 partitions can only store 50% of the files that can be stored on SLES10* [Technical Information Document 7009075]).

1.2.5 Ext4

In 2006, Ext4 started as a fork from Ext3. It eliminates some storage limitations of Ext3 by supporting volumes with a size of up to 1 exbibyte, files with a size of up to 16 tebibytes and an unlimited number of subdirectories. It also introduces several performance enhancements such as delayed block allocation and a much faster file system checking routine. Ext4 is also more reliable by supporting journal checksums and by providing time stamps measured in nanoseconds. Ext4 is fully backwards compatible to Ext2 and Ext3—both file systems can be mounted as Ext4.

1.2.6 ReiserFS

Officially one of the key features of the 2.4 kernel release, ReiserFS has been available as a kernel patch for 2.2.x SUSE kernels since version 6.4. ReiserFS was designed by Hans Reiser and the Namesys development team. It has proven itself to be a powerful alternative to Ext2. Its key assets are better disk space usage, better disk access performance, faster crash recovery, and reliability through data journaling.

 Important: Support of ReiserFS in SUSE Linux Enterprise Server 12

Existing ReiserFS partitions are supported for the lifetime of SUSE Linux Enterprise Server 12 specifically for migration purposes. Support for creating new ReiserFS file systems has been removed starting with SUSE Linux Enterprise Server 12.

1.2.6.1 Better Disk Space Usage

In ReiserFS, all data is organized in a structure called a B*-balanced tree. The tree structure contributes to better disk space usage because small files can be stored directly in the B* tree leaf nodes instead of being stored elsewhere and maintaining a pointer to the actual disk location. In addition to that, storage is not allocated in chunks of 1 or 4 KB, but in portions of the exact size needed. Another benefit lies in the dynamic allocation of inodes. This keeps the file system more flexible than traditional file systems, like Ext2, where the inode density must be specified at file system creation time.

1.2.6.2 Better Disk Access Performance

For small files, file data and "stat_data" (inode) information are often stored next to each other. They can be read with a single disk I/O operation, meaning that only one access to disk is required to retrieve all the information needed.

1.2.6.3 Fast Crash Recovery

Using a journal to keep track of recent metadata changes makes a file system check a matter of seconds, even for huge file systems.

1.2.6.4   Reliability through Data Journaling

ReiserFS also supports data journaling and ordered data modes similar to the concepts outlined in *Section 1.2.4, "Ext3"*. The default mode is `data=ordered`, which ensures both data and metadata integrity, but uses journaling only for metadata.

1.3   Other Supported File Systems

Table 1.1, "File System Types in Linux" summarizes some other file systems supported by Linux. They are supported mainly to ensure compatibility and interchange of data with different kinds of media or foreign operating systems.

TABLE 1.1: FILE SYSTEM TYPES IN LINUX

File System Type	Description
`cramfs`	Compressed ROM file system: A compressed read-only file system for ROMs.
`hpfs`	High Performance File System: The IBM OS/2 standard file system. Only supported in read-only mode.
`iso9660`	Standard file system on CD-ROMs.
`minix`	This file system originated from academic projects on operating systems and was the first file system used in Linux. Today, it is used as a file system for floppy disks.
`msdos`	`fat`, the file system originally used by DOS, is today used by various operating systems.
`ncpfs`	File system for mounting Novell volumes over networks.
`nfs`	Network File System: Here, data can be stored on any machine in a network and access might be granted via a network.
`ntfs`	Windows NT file system; read-only.
`smbfs`	Server Message Block is used by products such as Windows to enable file access over a network.

File System Type	Description
`sysv`	Used on SCO Unix, Xenix, and Coherent (commercial Unix systems for PCs).
`ufs`	Used by BSD, SunOS, and NextStep. Only supported in read-only mode.
`umsdos`	Unix on MS-DOS: Applied on top of a standard `fat` file system, achieves Unix functionality (permissions, links, long file names) by creating special files.
`vfat`	Virtual FAT: Extension of the `fat` file system (supports long file names).

1.4 Large File Support in Linux

Originally, Linux supported a maximum file size of 2 GiB (2^{31} bytes). Unless a file system comes with large file support, the maximum file size on a 32-bit system is 2 GiB.

Currently, all of our standard file systems have LFS (large file support), which gives a maximum file size of 2^{63} bytes in theory. *Table 1.2, "Maximum Sizes of Files and File Systems (On-Disk Format, 4 KiB Block Size)"* offers an overview of the current on-disk format limitations of Linux files and file systems. The numbers in the table assume that the file systems are using 4 KiB block size, which is a common standard. When using different block sizes, the results are different. The maximum file sizes in *Table 1.2, "Maximum Sizes of Files and File Systems (On-Disk Format, 4 KiB Block Size)"* can be larger than the file system's actual size when using sparse blocks.

 Note: Binary Multiples

In this document: 1024 Bytes = 1 KiB; 1024 KiB = 1 MiB; 1024 MiB = 1 GiB; 1024 GiB = 1 TiB; 1024 TiB = 1 PiB; 1024 PiB = 1 EiB (see also *NIST: Prefixes for Binary Multiples* [http://physics.nist.gov/cuu/Units/binary.html].

File System (4 KiB Block Size)	Maximum File System Size	Maximum File Size
Btrfs	16 EiB	16 EiB
Ext3	16 TiB	2 TiB
Ext4	1 EiB	16 TiB
OCFS2 (a cluster-aware file system available in the High Availability Extension)	16 TiB	1 EiB
ReiserFS v3.6	16 TiB	1 EiB
XFS	8 EiB	8 EiB
NFSv2 (client side)	8 EiB	2 GiB
NFSv3 (client side)	8 EiB	8 EiB

Important: Limitations

Table 1.2, "Maximum Sizes of Files and File Systems (On-Disk Format, 4 KiB Block Size)" describes the limitations regarding the on-disk format. The Linux kernel imposes its own limits on the size of files and file systems handled by it. These are as follows:

File Size

On 32-bit systems, files cannot exceed 2 TiB (2^{41} bytes).

File System Size

File systems can be up to 2^{73} bytes in size. However, this limit is still out of reach for the currently available hardware.

1.5 Linux Kernel Storage Limitations

Table 1.3, "Storage Limitations" summarizes the kernel limits for storage associated with SUSE Linux Enterprise Server.

TABLE 1.3: STORAGE LIMITATIONS

Storage Feature	Limitation
Maximum number of LUNs supported	16384 LUNs per target.
Maximum number of paths per single LUN	No limit by default. Each path is treated as a normal LUN. The actual limit is given by the number of LUNs per target and the number of targets per HBA (16777215 for a Fibre Channel HBA).
Maximum number of HBAs	Unlimited. The actual limit is determined by the amount of PCI slots of the system.
Maximum number of paths with device-mapper-multipath (in total) per operating system	Approximately 1024. The actual number depends on the length of the device number strings. It is a compile-time variable within multipath-tools, which can be raised if this limit poses a problem.
Maximum size per block device	Up to 8 EiB.

1.6 Troubleshooting File Systems

This section describes some known issues and possible solutions for file systems.

1.6.1 Btrfs Error: No space is left on device

The root (/) partition using the Btrfs file system stops accepting data. You receive the error "No space left on device".

See the following sections for information about possible causes and prevention of this issue.

1.6.1.1   Disk Space Consumed by Snapper Snapshots

If Snapper is running for the Btrfs file system, the "`No space left on device`" problem is typically caused by having too much data stored as snapshots on your system.

You can remove some snapshots from Snapper, however, the snapshots are not deleted immediately and might not free up as much space as you need.

To delete files from Snapper:

1. Open a terminal console.

2. At the command prompt, enter **btrfs filesystem show**, for example:

```
tux > sudo btrfs filesystem show
Label: none uuid: 40123456-cb2c-4678-8b3d-d014d1c78c78
 Total devices 1 FS bytes used 20.00GB
 devid 1 size 20.00GB used 20.00GB path /dev/sda3
```

3. Enter

```
sudo btrfs fi balance start mountpoint -dusage=5
```

This command attempts to relocate data in empty or near-empty data chunks, allowing the space to be reclaimed and reassigned to metadata. This can take a while (many hours for 1 TB) although the system is otherwise usable during this time.

4. List the snapshots in Snapper. Enter

```
sudo snapper -c root list
```

5. Delete one or more snapshots from Snapper. Enter

```
sudo snapper -c root delete snapshot_number(s)
```

Ensure that you delete the oldest snapshots first. The older a snapshot is, the more disk space it occupies.

To help prevent this problem, you can change the Snapper cleanup algorithms. See *Book "Administration Guide", Chapter 3 "System Recovery and Snapshot Management with Snapper", Section 3.5.1.2 "Cleanup-algorithms"* for details. The configuration values controlling snapshot cleanup are `EMPTY_*`, `NUMBER_*`, and `TIMELINE_*`.

If you use Snapper with Btrfs on the file system disk, it is advisable to reserve twice the amount of disk space than the standard storage proposal. The YaST Partitioner automatically proposes twice the standard disk space in the Btrfs storage proposal for the root file system.

1.6.1.2   Disk Space Consumed by Log, Crash, and Cache Files

If the system disk is filling up with data, you can try deleting files from `/var/log`, `/var/crash`, and `/var/cache`.

The Btrfs `root` file system subvolumes `/var/log`, `/var/crash` and `/var/cache` can use all of the available disk space during normal operation, and cause a system malfunction. To help avoid this situation, SUSE Linux Enterprise Server offers Btrfs quota support for subvolumes. See *Section 1.2.1.5, "Btrfs Quota Support for Subvolumes"* for details.

1.6.2   Freeing Unused Filesystem Blocks

On solid state drives (SSDs) and thinly provisioned volumes it is useful to trim blocks not in use by the file system. SUSE Linux Enterprise Server fully supports `unmap` or `trim` operations on all file systems supporting these methods.

The recommended way to trim a supported file system on SUSE Linux Enterprise Server is to run **/sbin/wiper.sh**. Make sure to read `/usr/share/doc/packages/hdparm/README.wiper` before running this script. For most desktop and server systems the sufficient trimming frequency is once a week. Mounting a file system with `-o discard` comes with a performance penalty and may negatively affect the lifetime of SSDs and is not recommended.

1.7 Additional Information

Each of the file system projects described above maintains its own home page on which to find mailing list information, further documentation, and FAQs:

- The Btrfs Wiki on Kernel.org: https://btrfs.wiki.kernel.org/

- E2fsprogs: Ext2/3/4 File System Utilities: http://e2fsprogs.sourceforge.net/

- Introducing Ext3: http://www.ibm.com/developerworks/linux/library/l-fs7/

- XFS: A High-Performance Journaling Filesytem: http://oss.sgi.com/projects/xfs/

- The OCFS2 Project: http://oss.oracle.com/projects/ocfs2/

A comprehensive multi-part tutorial about Linux file systems can be found at IBM developerWorks in the *Advanced File System Implementor's Guide* (https://www.ibm.com/developerworks/linux/library/l-fs/).

An in-depth comparison of file systems (not only Linux file systems) is available from the Wikipedia project in Comparison of File Systems (http://en.wikipedia.org/wiki/Comparison_of_file_systems#Comparison).

2 Resizing File Systems

Resizing file systems—not to be confused with resizing partitions or volumes—can be used to make space available on physical volumes or to use additional space available on a physical volume.

2.1 Use Cases

It is strongly recommended to use the YaST Partitioner to resize partitions or logical volumes. When doing so, the file system will automatically be adjusted to the new size of the partition or volume. However, there are some cases where you need to resize the file system manually, because they are not supported by YaST:

- After having resized a virtual disk of a VM Guest.

- After having resized a volume from a network-attached storage.

- After having manually resized partitions (for example by using **fdisk** or **parted**) or logical volumes (for example by using **lvresize**).

- When wanting to shrink Btrfs file systems (as of SUSE Linux Enterprise Server 12, YaST only supports growing Btrfs file systems).

2.2 Guidelines for Resizing

Resizing any file system involves some risks that can potentially result in losing data.

 Warning: Back Up your Data

To avoid data loss, ensure that you back up your data before you begin any resizing task.

Consider the following guidelines when planning to resize a file system.

2.2.1 File Systems that Support Resizing

The file system must support resizing to take advantage of increases in available space for the volume. In SUSE Linux Enterprise Server, file system resizing utilities are available for file systems Ext2, Ext3, Ext4, and ReiserFS. The utilities support increasing and decreasing the size as follows:

TABLE 2.1: FILE SYSTEM SUPPORT FOR RESIZING

File System	Utility	Increase Size (Grow)	Decrease Size (Shrink)
Btrfs	`btrfs filesystem resize`	Online	Online
XFS	`xfs_growfs`	Online	Not supported
Ext2	`resize2fs`	Offline only	Offline only
Ext3	`resize2fs`	Online or offline	Offline only
Ext4	`resize2fs`	Offline only	Offline only
ReiserFS	`resize_reiserfs`	Online or offline	Offline only

2.2.2 Increasing the Size of a File System

You can grow a file system to the maximum space available on the device, or specify an exact size. Ensure that you grow the size of the device or logical volume before you attempt to increase the size of the file system.

When specifying an exact size for the file system, ensure that the new size satisfies the following conditions:

* The new size must be greater than the size of the existing data; otherwise, data loss occurs.

* The new size must be equal to or less than the current device size because the file system size cannot extend beyond the space available.

2.2.3　Decreasing the Size of a File System

When decreasing the size of the file system on a device, ensure that the new size satisfies the following conditions:

- The new size must be greater than the size of the existing data; otherwise, data loss occurs.

- The new size must be equal to or less than the current device size because the file system size cannot extend beyond the space available.

If you plan to also decrease the size of the logical volume that holds the file system, ensure that you decrease the size of the file system before you attempt to decrease the size of the device or logical volume.

 Important: XFS

Decreasing the size of a file system formatted with XFS is not possible, since such a feature is not supported by XFS.

2.3　Changing the Size of a Btrfs File System

The size of a Btrfs file system can be changed by using the **btrfs filesystem resize** command when the file system is mounted. Increasing and decreasing the size are both supported while the file system is mounted.

1. Open a terminal console.

2. Make sure the file system you want to change is mounted.

3. Change the size of the file system using the **btrfs filesystem resize** command with one of the following methods:

   - To extend the file system size to the maximum available size of the device, enter

   ```
   sudo btrfs filesystem resize max /mnt
   ```

   - To extend the file system to a specific size, enter

   ```
   sudo btrfs filesystem resize size /mnt
   ```

Replace *size* with the desired size in bytes. You can also specify units on the value, such as 50000K (kilobytes), 250M (megabytes), or 2G (gigabytes). Alternatively, you can specify an increase or decrease to the current size by prefixing the value with a plus (+) or a minus (-) sign, respectively:

```
sudo btrfs filesystem resize +size /mnt
sudo btrfs filesystem resize -size /mnt
```

4. Check the effect of the resize on the mounted file system by entering

```
df -h
```

The Disk Free (**df**) command shows the total size of the disk, the number of blocks used, and the number of blocks available on the file system. The -h option prints sizes in human-readable format, such as 1K, 234M, or 2G.

2.4 Changing the Size of an XFS File System

The size of an XFS file system can be increased by using the **xfs_growfs** command when the file system is mounted. Reducing the size of an XFS file system is not possible.

1. Open a terminal console.

2. Make sure the file system you want to change is mounted.

3. Increase the size of the file system using the **xfs_growfs** command. The following example expands the size of the file system to the maximum value available. See **man 8 xfs_growfs** for more options.

```
sudo xfs_growfs -d /mnt
```

4. Check the effect of the resize on the mounted file system by entering

```
df -h
```

The Disk Free (**df**) command shows the total size of the disk, the number of blocks used, and the number of blocks available on the file system. The -h option prints sizes in human-readable format, such as 1K, 234M, or 2G.

2.5 Changing the Size of an Ext2, Ext3, or Ext4 File System

The size of Ext2, Ext3, and Ext4 file systems can be increased by using the **resize2fs** command when the file system is mounted. The size of an Ext3 file system can also be increased by using the **resize2fs** command when the file system is unmounted. To decrease the size of an Ext file system it needs to be unmounted.

1. Open a terminal console.

2. If the file system is Ext2, you must unmount the file system in any case. The Ext3 and Ext4 file systems can be mounted for increasing the size; they need to be unmounted for decreasing the size.

3. Change the size of the file system using one of the following methods:

   - To extend the file system size to the maximum available size of the device called `/dev/sda1`, enter

     ```
     sudo resize2fs /dev/sda1
     ```

     If a size parameter is not specified, the size defaults to the size of the partition.

   - To change the file system to a specific size, enter

     ```
     sudo resize2fs /dev/sda1 size
     ```

     The `size` parameter specifies the requested new size of the file system. If no units are specified, the unit of the size parameter is the block size of the file system. Optionally, the size parameter can be suffixed by one of the following unit designators: `s` for 512 byte sectors; `K` for kilobytes (1 kilobyte is 1024 bytes); `M` for megabytes; or `G` for gigabytes.

   Wait until the resizing is completed before continuing.

4. If the file system is not mounted, mount it now.

5. Check the effect of the resize on the mounted file system by entering

   ```
   df -h
   ```

The Disk Free (**df**) command shows the total size of the disk, the number of blocks used, and the number of blocks available on the file system. The -h option prints sizes in human-readable format, such as 1K, 234M, or 2G.

2.6   Changing the Size of a Reiser File System

A ReiserFS file system can be increased in size while mounted or unmounted. To decrease its size it needs to be unmounted.

1. Open a terminal console.

2. If you want to decrease the size of the file system, unmount it in case it is mounted.

3. Change the size of the file system on the device called /dev/sda2, using one of the following methods:

   * To extend the file system size to the maximum available size of the device, enter

     ```
     sudo resize_reiserfs /dev/sda2
     ```

     When no size is specified, this increases the volume to the full size of the partition.

   * To extend the file system to a specific size, enter

     ```
     sudo resize_reiserfs -s size /dev/sda2
     ```

     Replace *size* with the desired size in bytes. You can also specify units on the value, such as 50000K (kilobytes), 250M (megabytes), or 2G (gigabytes). Alternatively, you can specify an increase or decrease to the current size by prefixing the value with a plus (+) or minus (-) sign, respectively:

     ```
     sudo resize_reiserfs -s +size /dev/sda2
     sudo resize_reiserfs -s -size /dev/sda2
     ```

   Wait until the resizing is completed before continuing.

4. If the file system is not mounted, mount it now.

5. Check the effect of the resize on the mounted file system by entering

```
df -h
```

The Disk Free (**df**) command shows the total size of the disk, the number of blocks used, and the number of blocks available on the file system. The -h option prints sizes in human-readable format, such as 1K, 234M, or 2G.

Changing the Size of a Reiser File System

3 Using UUIDs to Mount Devices

This section describes the use of UUIDs (Universally Unique Identifiers) instead of device names (such as `/dev/sda1`) to identify file system devices. Starting with SUSE Linux Enterprise Server 12, UUIDs are used by default in the boot loader file and the `/etc/fstab` file.

3.1 Persistent Device Names with udev

Since Kernel 2.6, **udev** provides a userspace solution for the dynamic `/dev` directory, with persistent device naming. As part of the hotplug system, **udev** is executed if a device is added to or removed from the system.

A list of rules is used to match against specific device attributes. The **udev** rules infrastructure (defined in the `/etc/udev/rules.d` directory) provides stable names for all disk devices, regardless of their order of recognition or the connection used for the device. The **udev** tools examine every appropriate block device that the kernel creates to apply naming rules based on certain buses, drive types, or file systems. For information about how to define your own rules for **udev**, see *Writing udev Rules* [http://reactivated.net/writing_udev_rules.html].

Along with the dynamic kernel-provided device node name, **udev** maintains classes of persistent symbolic links pointing to the device in the `/dev/disk` directory, which is further categorized by the `by-id`, `by-label`, `by-path`, and `by-uuid` subdirectories.

 Note: UUID Generators

Other programs besides **udev**, such as LVM or **md**, might also generate UUIDs, but they are not listed in `/dev/disk`.

3.2 Understanding UUIDs

A UUID (Universally Unique Identifier) is a 128-bit number for a file system that is unique on both the local system and across other systems. It is randomly generated with system hardware information and time stamps as part of its seed. UUIDs are commonly used to uniquely tag devices.

Using non-persistent "traditional" device names such as `/dev/sda1` may render the system unbootable when adding storage. For example, if root (`/`) is assigned to `/dev/sda1`, it might be reassigned to `/dev/sdg1` after a SAN has been attached or additional hard disks have been applied to the system. In this case the boot loader configuration and the `/etc/fstab` file need to be adjusted, otherwise the system will no longer boot.

One way to avoid this problem is to use the UUID in the boot loader and `/etc/fstab` files for the boot device. This is the default in SUSE Linux Enterprise since version 12. The UUID is a property of the file system and can change if you reformat the drive. Other alternatives to using UUIDs of device names would be to identify devices by ID or label.

You can also use the UUID as criterion for assembling and activating software RAID devices. When a RAID is created, the **md** driver generates a UUID for the device, and stores the value in the `md` superblock.

You can find the UUID for any block device in the `/dev/disk/by-uuid` directory. For example, a UUID entry looks like this:

```
tux > ls -og /dev/disk/by-uuid/
lrwxrwxrwx 1 10 Dec  5 07:48 e014e482-1c2d-4d09-84ec-61b3aefde77a -> ../../sda1
```

3.3 Additional Information

For more information about using `udev` for managing devices, see *Book "Administration Guide", Chapter 15 "Dynamic Kernel Device Management with* udev*"*.

For more information about `udev` commands, see **man 7 udev**.

II Logical Volumes (LVM)

4 LVM Configuration

This chapter briefly describes the principles behind Logical Volume Manager (LVM) and its basic features that make it useful under many circumstances. The YaST LVM configuration can be reached from the YaST Expert Partitioner. This partitioning tool enables you to edit and delete existing partitions and create new ones that should be used with LVM.

 Warning: Risks

Using LVM might be associated with increased risk, such as data loss. Risks also include application crashes, power failures, and faulty commands. Save your data before implementing LVM or reconfiguring volumes. Never work without a backup.

4.1 Understanding the Logical Volume Manager

LVM enables flexible distribution of hard disk space over several physical volumes (hard disks, partitions, LUNs). It was developed because the need to change the segmentation of hard disk space might arise only after the initial partitioning has already been done during installation. Because it is difficult to modify partitions on a running system, LVM provides a virtual pool (volume group or VG) of storage space from which logical volumes (LVs) can be created as needed. The operating system accesses these LVs instead of the physical partitions. Volume groups can span more than one disk, so that several disks or parts of them can constitute one single VG. In this way, LVM provides a kind of abstraction from the physical disk space that allows its segmentation to be changed in a much easier and safer way than through physical repartitioning.

Figure 4.1, "Physical Partitioning versus LVM" compares physical partitioning (left) with LVM segmentation (right). On the left side, one single disk has been divided into three physical partitions (PART), each with a mount point (MP) assigned so that the operating system can access them. On the right side, two disks have been divided into two and three physical partitions each. Two LVM volume groups (VG 1 and VG 2) have been defined. VG 1 contains two partitions from DISK 1 and one from DISK 2. VG 2 contains the remaining two partitions from DISK 2.

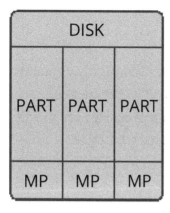

FIGURE 4.1: PHYSICAL PARTITIONING VERSUS LVM

In LVM, the physical disk partitions that are incorporated in a volume group are called physical volumes (PVs). Within the volume groups in *Figure 4.1, "Physical Partitioning versus LVM"*, four logical volumes (LV 1 through LV 4) have been defined, which can be used by the operating system via the associated mount points (MP). The border between different logical volumes need not be aligned with any partition border. See the border between LV 1 and LV 2 in this example.

LVM features:

- Several hard disks or partitions can be combined in a large logical volume.

- Provided the configuration is suitable, an LV (such as /usr) can be enlarged when the free space is exhausted.

- Using LVM, it is possible to add hard disks or LVs in a running system. However, this requires hotpluggable hardware that is capable of such actions.

- It is possible to activate a *striping mode* that distributes the data stream of a logical volume over several physical volumes. If these physical volumes reside on different disks, this can improve the reading and writing performance like RAID 0.

- The snapshot feature enables consistent backups (especially for servers) in the running system.

With these features, using LVM already makes sense for heavily used home PCs or small servers. If you have a growing data stock, as in the case of databases, music archives, or user directories, LVM is especially useful. It allows file systems that are larger than the physical hard disk. However, keep in mind that working with LVM is different from working with conventional partitions.

Understanding the Logical Volume Manager

You can manage new or existing LVM storage objects by using the YaST Partitioner. Instructions and further information about configuring LVM are available in the official *LVM HOWTO* [http://tldp.org/HOWTO/LVM-HOWTO/].

 Important: Adding Multipath Support upon an Existing LVM Configuration

If you add multipath support after you have configured LVM, you must modify the `/etc/lvm/lvm.conf` file to scan only the multipath device names in the `/dev/disk/by-id` directory as described in *Section 15.12, "Using LVM2 on Multipath Devices"*, then reboot the server.

4.2   Creating Volume Groups

An LVM volume group (VG) organizes the Linux LVM partitions into a logical pool of space. You can carve out logical volumes from the available space in the group. The Linux LVM partitions in a group can be on the same or different disks. You can add partitions or entire disks to expand the size of the group. If you want to use an entire disk, it must not contain any partitions. If using partitions, they must not be mounted. YaST will automatically change their partition type to `0x8E Linux LVM` when adding them to a VG.

1. Launch YaST and open the *Partitioner*.

2. In case you need to reconfigure your existing partitioning setup, proceed as follows. Refer to *Book "Deployment Guide", Chapter 14 "Advanced Disk Setup", Section 14.1 "Using the YaST Partitioner"* for details. Skip this step if you only want to use unused disks or partitions that already exist.

   a. To use an entire hard disk that already contains partitions, delete all partitions on that disk.

   b. To use a partition that is currently mounted, unmount it.

   c. To use unpartitioned, free space on a hard disk, create a new primary or logical partition on that disk. Set its type to `0x8E Linux LVM`. Do not format or mount it.

3. In the left panel, select *Volume Management.*

A list of existing Volume Groups opens in the right panel.

4. At the lower left of the Volume Management page, click *Add › Volume Group.*

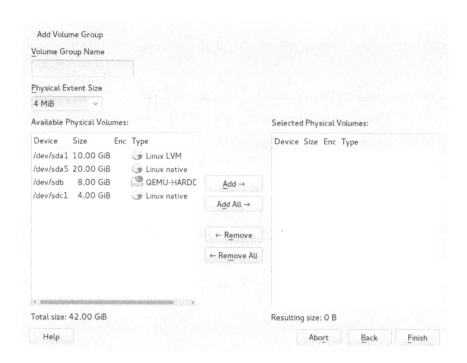

5. Define the volume group as follows:

   a. Specify the *Volume Group Name.*

   If you are creating a volume group at install time, the name `system` is suggested for a volume group that will contain the SUSE Linux Enterprise Server system files.

   b. Specify the *Physical Extent Size.*

   The *Physical Extent Size* defines the size of a physical block in the volume group. All the disk space in a volume group is handled in chunks of this size. Values can be from 1 KB to 16 GB in powers of 2. This value is normally set to 4 MB.

   In LVM1, a 4 MB physical extent allowed a maximum LV size of 256 GB because it supports only up to 65534 extents per LV. LVM2, which is used on SUSE Linux Enterprise Server, does not restrict the number of physical extents. Having many extents has no impact on I/O performance to the logical volume, but it slows down the LVM tools.

Important: Physical Extent Sizes

Different physical extent sizes should not be mixed in a single VG. The extent should not be modified after the initial setup.

c. In the *Available Physical Volumes* list, select the Linux LVM partitions that you want to make part of this volume group, then click *Add* to move them to the *Selected Physical Volumes* list.

d. Click *Finish*.

The new group appears in the *Volume Groups* list.

6. On the Volume Management page, click *Next*, verify that the new volume group is listed, then click *Finish*.

7. To check which physical devices are part of the volume group, open the YaST Partitioner at any time in the running system and click *Volume Management* › *Edit* › *Physical Devices*. Leave this screen with *Abort*.

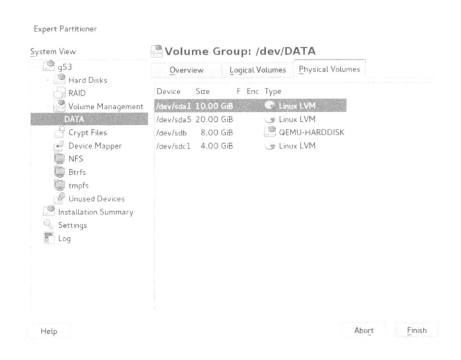

FIGURE 4.2: PHYSICAL VOLUMES IN THE VOLUME GROUP NAMED DATA

4.3 Creating Logical Volumes

A logical volume provides a pool of space similar to what a hard disk does. To make this space usable, you need to define logical volumes. A logical volume is similar to a regular partition—you can format and mount it.

Use The YaST Partitioner to create logical volumes from an existing volume group. Assign at least one logical volume to each volume group. You can create new logical volumes as needed until all free space in the volume group has been exhausted. An LVM logical volume can optionally be thinly provisioned allowing you to create logical volumes with sizes that overbook the available free space (see *Section 4.3.1, "Thinly Provisioned Logical Volumes"* for more information).

- **Normal volume:** (Default) The volume's space is allocated immediately.

- **Thin pool:** The logical volume is a pool of space that is reserved for use with thin volumes. The thin volumes can allocate their needed space from it on demand.

- **Thin volume:** The volume is created as a sparse volume. The volume allocates needed space on demand from a thin pool.

PROCEDURE 4.1: SETTING UP A LOGICAL VOLUME

1. Launch YaST and open the *Partitioner*.

2. In the left panel, select *Volume Management*. A list of existing Volume Groups opens in the right panel.

3. Select the volume group in which you want to create the volume and choose *Add › Logical Volume*.

4. Provide a *Name* for the volume and choose *Normal Volume* (refer to *Section 4.3.1, "Thinly Provisioned Logical Volumes"* for setting up thinly provisioned volumes). Proceed with *Next*.

Add Logical Volume on /dev/DATA

Name

Logical Volume

LOCAL

Type

◉ Normal Volume

○ Thin Pool

○ Thin Volume

Used Pool

| Help | | Abort | Back | Next |

5. Specify the size of the volume and whether to use multiple stripes.

Using a striped volume, the data will be distributed among several physical volumes. If these physical volumes reside on different hard disks, this generally results in a better reading and writing performance (like RAID 0). The maximum number of available stripes is equal to the number of physical volumes. The default (1 is to not use multiple stripes.

6. Choose a *Role* for the volume. Your choice here only affects the default values for the upcoming dialog. They can be changed in the next step. If in doubt, choose *Raw Volume (Unformatted)*.

7. Under *Formatting Options*, select *Format Partition*, then select the *File system*. The content of the *Options* menu depends on the file system. Usually there is no need to change the defaults.

   Under *Mounting Options*, select *Mount partition*, then select the mount point. Click *Fstab Options* to add special mounting options for the volume.

8. Click *Finish*.

9. Click *Next*, verify that the changes are listed, then click *Finish*.

4.3.1   Thinly Provisioned Logical Volumes

An LVM logical volume can optionally be thinly provisioned. Thin provisioning allows you to create logical volumes with sizes that overbook the available free space. You create a thin pool that contains unused space reserved for use with an arbitrary number of thin volumes. A thin volume is created as a sparse volume and space is allocated from a thin pool as needed. The thin pool can be expanded dynamically when needed for cost-effective allocation of storage space. Thinly provisioned volumes also support snapshots which can be managed with Snapper—see *Book "Administration Guide", Chapter 3 "System Recovery and Snapshot Management with Snapper"* for more information.

To set up a thinly provisioned logical volume, proceed as described in *Procedure 4.1, "Setting Up a Logical Volume"*. When it comes to choosing the volume type, do not choose *Normal Volume*, but rather *Thin Volume* or *Thin Pool*.

Thin pool

   The logical volume is a pool of space that is reserved for use with thin volumes. The thin volumes can allocate their needed space from it on demand.

Thin volume

   The volume is created as a sparse volume. The volume allocates needed space on demand from a thin pool.

> **Important: Thinly Provisioned Volumes in a Cluster**
>
> To use thinly provisioned volumes in a cluster, the thin pool and the thin volumes that use it must be managed in a single cluster resource. This allows the thin volumes and thin pool to always be mounted exclusively on the same node.

4.4 Automatically Activating Non-Root LVM Volume Groups

Activation behavior for non-root LVM volume groups is controlled in the `/etc/lvm/lvm.conf` file and by the `auto_activation_volume_list` parameter. By default, the parameter is empty and all volumes are activated. To activate only some volume groups, add the names in quotes and separate them with commas, for example:

```
auto_activation_volume_list = [ "vg1", "vg2/lvol1", "@tag1", "@*" ]
```

If you have defined a list in the `auto_activation_volume_list` parameter, the following will happen:

1. Each logical volume is first checked against this list.

2. If it does not match, the logical volume will not be activated.

By default, non-root LVM volume groups are automatically activated on system restart by Dracut. This parameter allows you to activate all volume groups on system restart, or to activate only specified non-root LVM volume groups.

4.5 Resizing an Existing Volume Group

The space provided by a volume group can be expanded at any time in the running system without service interruption by adding more physical volumes. This will allow you to add logical volumes to the group or to expand the size of existing volumes as described in *Section 4.6, "Resizing a Logical Volume"*.

It is also possible to reduce the size of the volume group by removing physical volumes. YaST only allows to remove physical volumes that are currently unused. To find out which physical volumes are currently in use, run the following command. The partitions (physical volumes) listed in the `PE Ranges` column are the ones in use:

```
tux > sudo pvs -o vg_name,lv_name,pv_name,seg_pe_ranges
root's password:
  VG   LV    PV          PE Ranges
              /dev/sda1
  DATA DEVEL /dev/sda5   /dev/sda5:0-3839
```

```
DATA        /dev/sda5
DATA LOCAL /dev/sda6   /dev/sda6:0-2559
DATA        /dev/sda7
DATA        /dev/sdb1
DATA        /dev/sdc1
```

1. Launch YaST and open the *Partitioner*.

2. In the left panel, select *Volume Management*. A list of existing Volume Groups opens in the right panel.

3. Select the volume group you want to change, then click *Resize*.

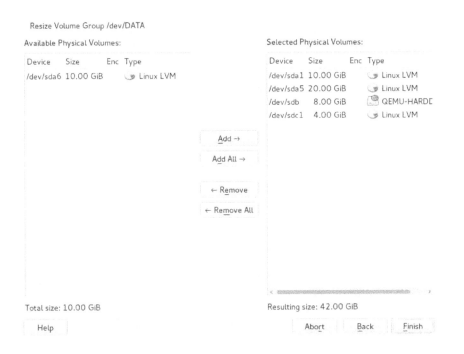

4. Do one of the following:

   • **Add:** Expand the size of the volume group by moving one or more physical volumes (LVM partitions) from the *Available Physical Volumes* list to the *Selected Physical Volumes* list.

   • **Remove:** Reduce the size of the volume group by moving one or more physical volumes (LVM partitions) from the *Selected Physical Volumes* list to the *Available Physical Volumes* list.

5. Click *Finish.*

6. Click *Next,* verify that the changes are listed, then click *Finish.*

4.6   Resizing a Logical Volume

In case there is unused free space available in the volume group, you can enlarge a logical volume to provide more usable space. You may also reduce the size of a volume to free space in the volume group that can be used by other logical volumes.

 Note: "Online" Resizing

When reducing the size of a volume, YaST automatically resizes its file system, too. Whether a volume that is currently mounted can be resized "online" (that is while being mounted), depends on its file system. Growing the file system online is supported by Btrfs, XFS, Ext3, and ReiserFS.

Shrinking the file system online is only supported by Btrfs. To shrink XFS, Ext2/3/4, and ReiserFS volumes, you need to unmount them. Shrinking volumes formatted with XFS is not possible, since XFS does not support file system shrinking.

1. Launch YaST and open the *Partitioner.*

2. In the left panel, select *Volume Management.* A list of existing Volume Groups opens in the right panel.

3. Select the logical volume you want to change, then click *Resize.*

Resize Logical Volume /dev/DATA/LOCAL

Size

⦿ Maximum Size (51.98 GiB)

◯ Minimum Size (266.00 MiB)

◯ Custom Size

Size

15.00 GiB

Current size: 15.00 GiB

| Help | | Cancel | OK |

4. Set the intended size by using one of the following options:

- **Maximum Size.** Expand the size of the logical volume to use all space left in the volume group.

- **Minimum Size.** Reduce the size of the logical volume to the size occupied by the data and the file system metadata.

- **Custom Size.** Specify the new size for the volume. The value must be within the range of the minimum and maximum values listed above. Use K, M, G, T for Kilobytes, Megabytes, Gigabytes and Terabytes (for example 20G).

5. Click *OK*.

6. Click *Next*, verify that the change is listed, then click *Finish*.

4.7 Deleting a Volume Group or a Logical Volume

🛑 **Warning: Data Loss**

Deleting a volume group destroys all of the data in each of its member partitions. Deleting a logical volume destroys all data stored on the volume.

1. Launch YaST and open the *Partitioner*.

2. In the left panel, select *Volume Management*. A list of existing volume groups opens in the right panel.

3. Select the volume group or the logical volume you want to remove and click *Delete*.

4. Depending on your choice warning dialogs are shown. Confirm them with *Yes*.

5. Click *Next*, verify that the deleted volume group is listed (deletion is indicated by a red colored font), then click *Finish*.

4.8 Using LVM Commands

For information about using LVM commands, see the man pages for the commands described in the following table. All commands need to be executed with `root` privileges. Either use **sudo** `command` (recommended) or execute them directly as `root`.

TABLE 4.1: LVM COMMANDS

Command	Description
`pvcreate device`	Initializes a device (such as `/dev/sdb`) for use by LVLM as a physical volume.
`pvdisplay device`	Displays information about the LVM physical volume, such as whether it is currently being used in a logical volume.

Command	Description
`vgcreate -c y vg_name dev1 [dev2...]`	Creates a clustered volume group with one or more specified devices.
`vgchange -a [ey|n] vg_name`	Activates (`-a ey`) or deactivates (`-a n`) a volume group and its logical volumes for input/output. When activationg a volume in a cluster, ensure that you use the `ey` option. This option is used by default in the load script.
`vgremove vg_name`	Removes a volume group. Before using this command, remove the logical volumes, then deactivate the volume group.
`vgdisplay vg_name`	Displays information about a specified volume group. To find the total physical extent of a volume group, enter `vgdisplay vg_name | grep "Total PE"`
`lvcreate -L size -n lv_name vg_name`	Creates a logical volume of the specified size.
`lvcreate -L size --thinpool pool_name vg_name`	Creates a thin pool named `my-Pool` of the specified size from the volume group `vg_name`.

Command	Description
	The following example creates a thin pool with a size of 5 GB from the volume group `LOCAL`: **`lvcreate -L 5G --thinpool myPool LOCAL`**

`lvcreate -T`
`vg_name/pool_name -V size \`
`-n lv_name`
	Creates a thin logical volume within the pool *pool_name*. The following example creates a 1GB thin volume named `myThin1` from the pool `myPool` on the volume group `LOCAL`: **`lvcreate -T LOCAL/myPool -V 1G -n myThin1`**

`lvcreate -T vg_name/pool_name -V size -L size \` `-n LV_name`	It is also possible to combine thin pool and thin logical volume creation in one command: **`lvcreate -T LOCAL/myPool -V 1G -L 5G -n myThin1`**
`lvcreate -s [-L size] -n snap_volume \` `source_volume_path vg_name`	Creates a snapshot volume for the specified logical volume. If the size option (`-L` or `--size`) is not included, the snapshot is created as a thin snapshot.
`lvremove /dev/vg_name/lv_name`	Removes a logical volume. Before using this command, close the logical volume by dismounting it with the **`umount`** command.
`lvremove snap_volume_path`	Removes a snapshot volume.

Command	Description
`lvconvert --merge` *`snap_volume_path`*	Reverts the logical volume to the version of the snapshot.
`vgextend` *`vg_name device`*	Adds the specified device (physical volume) to an existing volume group.
`vgreduce` *`vg_name device`*	Removes a specified physical volume from an existing volume group. Ensure that the physical volume is not currently being used by a logical volume. If it is, you must move the data to another physical volume by using the **pvmove** command.
`lvextend -L` *`size`* `/dev/`*`vg_name`*`/`*`lv_name`*	Extends the size of a specified logical volume. Afterwards, you must also expand the file system to take advantage of the newly available space. See *Chapter 2, Resizing File Systems* for details.
`lvreduce -L` *`size`* `/dev/`*`vg_name`*`/`*`lv_name`*	Reduces the size of a specified logical volume. Ensure that you reduce the size of the file system first before shrinking the volume, otherwise you risk losing data. See *Chapter 2, Resizing File Systems* for details.

Command	Description
`lvrename /dev/`*`vg_name`*`/`*`lv_name`* `\` `/dev/`*`vg_name`*`/`*`new_lv_name`*	Renames an existing LVM logical volume. It does not change the volume group name.

 Tip: Bypassing udev on Volume Creation

In case that you want use LVM to manage LV device nodes and symbolic links instead of by udev rules, you can achieve this by disabling notifications from udev with one of the following methods:

- Configure `activation/udev_rules = 0` and `activation/udev_sync = 0` in `/etc/lvm/lvm.conf`.
  Note that specifying `--nodevsync` with the **lvcreate** command has the same affect as `activation/udev_sync = 0`; setting `activation/udev_rules = 0` is still required.

- Setting the environment variable `DM_DISABLE_UDEV`:

```
export DM_DISABLE_UDEV=1
```

This will also disable notifications from udev. In addition, all udev related settings from `/etc/lvm/lvm.conf` will be ignored.

4.8.1   Resizing a Logical Volume with Commands

The **lvresize**, **lvextend**, and **lvreduce** commands are used to resize logical volumes. See the man pages for each of these commands for syntax and options information. To extend an LV there must be enough unallocated space available on the VG.

The recommended way to grow or shrink a logical volume is to use the YaST Partitioner. When using YaST, the size of the file system in the volume will automatically be adjusted, too.

LVs can be extended or shrunk manually while they are being used, but this may not be true for a file system on them. Extending or shrinking the LV does not automatically modify the size of file systems in the volume. You must use a different command to grow the file system afterwards. For information about resizing file systems, see *Chapter 2, Resizing File Systems*.

Ensure that you use the right sequence when manually resizing an LV:

- If you extend an LV, you must extend the LV before you attempt to grow the file system.

- If you shrink an LV, you must shrink the file system before you attempt to shrink the LV.

To extend the size of a logical volume:

1. Open a terminal console.

2. If the logical volume contains an Ext2 or Ext4 file system, which do not support online growing, dismount it. In case it contains file systems that are hosted for a virtual machine (such as a Xen VM), shut down the VM first.

3. At the terminal console prompt, enter the following command to grow the size of the logical volume:

   ```
   sudo lvextend -L +size /dev/vg_name/lv_name
   ```

   For *size*, specify the amount of space you want to add to the logical volume, such as 10 GB. Replace */dev/vg_name/lv_name* with the Linux path to the logical volume, such as /dev/LOCAL/DATA. For example:

   ```
   sudo lvextend -L +10GB /dev/vg1/v1
   ```

4. Adjust the size of the file system. See *Chapter 2, Resizing File Systems* for details.

5. In case you have dismounted the file system, mount it again.

For example, to extend an LV with a (mounted and active) Btrfs on it by 10 GB:

```
sudo lvextend -L +10G /dev/LOCAL/DATA
sudo btrfs filesystem resize +10G /dev/LOCAL/DATA
```

To shrink the size of a logical volume:

1. Open a terminal console.

2. If the logical volume does not contain a Btrfs file system, dismount it. In case it contains file systems that are hosted for a virtual machine (such as a Xen VM), shut down the VM first. Note that volumes with the XFS file system cannot be reduced in size.

3. Adjust the size of the file system. See *Chapter 2, Resizing File Systems* for details.

4. At the terminal console prompt, enter the following command to shrink the size of the logical volume to the size of the file system:

```
sudo lvreduce /dev/vg_name/lv_name
```

5. In case you have unmounted the file system, mount it again.

For example, to shrink an LV with a Btrfs on it by 5 GB:

```
sudo btrfs filesystem resize -size 5G /dev/LOCAL/DATA
sudo lvreduce /dev/LOCAL/DATA
```

 ## Tip: Resizing the Volume and the File System with a Single Command

Starting with SUSE Linux Enterprise Server 12 SP1, **lvextend**, **lvresize**, and **lvreduce** support the option `--resizefs` that will not only change the size of the volume, but will also resize the file system. Therefore the examples for **lvextend** and **lvreduce** shown above, can alternatively be run as follows:

```
sudo lvextend --resizefs −L +10G /dev/LOCAL/DATA
sudo lvreduce  --resizefs -L -5G /dev/LOCAL/DATA
```

Note that the `--resizefs` is supported for the following file systems: ext2/3/4, reiserfs, Btrfs, XFS. Resizing Btrfs with this option is currently only available on SUSE Linux Enterprise Server, since is not yet accepted upstream.

Resizing a Logical Volume with Commands

4.8.2 Dynamic Aggregation of LVM Metadata via `lvmetad`

Most LVM commands require an accurate view of the LVM metadata stored on the disk devices in the system. With the current LVM design, if this information is not available, LVM must scan all the physical disk devices in the system. This requires a significant amount of I/O operations in systems that have a large number of disks. In case a disk fails to respond, LVM commands might run into a timeout while waiting for the disk.

Dynamic aggregation of LVM metadata via `lvmetad` provides a solution for this problem. The purpose of the `lvmetad` daemon is to eliminate the need for this scanning by dynamically aggregating metadata information each time the status of a device changes. These events are signaled to `lvmetad` by udev rules. If the daemon is not running, LVM performs a scan as it normally would do.

This feature is enabled by default. In case it is disabled on your system, proceed as follows to enable it:

1. Open a terminal console.

2. Stop the `lvmetad` daemon:

   ```
   sudo systemctl stop lvm2-lvmetad
   ```

3. Edit `/etc/lvm/lvm.conf` and set `use_lvmetad` to `1`:

   ```
   use_lvmetad = 1
   ```

4. Restart the `lvmetad` daemon:

   ```
   sudo systemctl start lvm2-lvmetad
   ```

4.9 Tagging LVM2 Storage Objects

A tag is an unordered keyword or term assigned to the metadata of a storage object. Tagging allows you to classify collections of LVM storage objects in ways that you find useful by attaching an unordered list of tags to their metadata.

4.9.1 Using LVM2 Tags

After you tag the LVM2 storage objects, you can use the tags in commands to accomplish the following tasks:

- Select LVM objects for processing according to the presence or absence of specific tags.

- Use tags in the configuration file to control which volume groups and logical volumes are activated on a server.

- Override settings in a global configuration file by specifying tags in the command.

A tag can be used in place of any command line LVM object reference that accepts:

- a list of objects

- a single object as long as the tag expands to a single object

Replacing the object name with a tag is not supported everywhere yet. After the arguments are expanded, duplicate arguments in a list are resolved by removing the duplicate arguments, and retaining the first instance of each argument.

Wherever there might be ambiguity of argument type, you must prefix a tag with the commercial at sign (@) character, such as `@mytag`. Elsewhere, using the "@" prefix is optional.

4.9.2 Requirements for Creating LVM2 Tags

Consider the following requirements when using tags with LVM:

Supported Characters

An LVM tag word can contain the ASCII uppercase characters A to Z, lowercase characters a to z, numbers 0 to 9, underscore (_), plus (+), hyphen (-), and period (.). The word cannot begin with a hyphen. The maximum length is 128 characters.

Supported Storage Objects

You can tag LVM2 physical volumes, volume groups, logical volumes, and logical volume segments. PV tags are stored in its volume group's metadata. Deleting a volume group also deletes the tags in the orphaned physical volume. Snapshots cannot be tagged, but their origin can be tagged.

LVM1 objects cannot be tagged because the disk format does not support it.

4.9.3   Command Line Tag Syntax

--addtag *tag_info*

Add a tag to (or *tag*) an LVM2 storage object. Example:

```
sudo vgchange --addtag @db1 vg1
```

--deltag *tag_info*

Remove a tag from (or *untag*) an LVM2 storage object. Example:

```
sudo vgchange --deltag @db1 vg1
```

--tag *tag_info*

Specify the tag to use to narrow the list of volume groups or logical volumes to be activated or deactivated.

Enter the following to activate the volume if it has a tag that matches the tag provided (example):

```
sudo lvchange -ay --tag @db1 vg1/vol2
```

4.9.4   Configuration File Syntax

4.9.4.1   Enabling Host Name Tags in the lvm.conf File

Add the following code to the /etc/lvm/lvm.conf file to enable host tags that are defined separately on host in a /etc/lvm/lvm_<hostname>.conf file.

```
tags {
    # Enable hostname tags
    hosttags = 1
}
```

You place the activation code in the /etc/lvm/lvm_<hostname>.conf file on the host. See *Section 4.9.4.3, "Defining Activation"*.

4.9.4.2 Defining Tags for Host Names in the lvm.conf File

```
tags {

  tag1 { }
    # Tag does not require a match to be set.

  tag2 {
    # If no exact match, tag is not set.
    host_list = [ "hostname1", "hostname2" ]
  }
}
```

4.9.4.3 Defining Activation

You can modify the /etc/lvm/lvm.conf file to activate LVM logical volumes based on tags. In a text editor, add the following code to the file:

```
activation {
    volume_list = [ "vg1/lvol0", "@database" ]
}
```

Replace @database with your tag. Use "@*" to match the tag against any tag set on the host.

The activation command matches against *vgname*, *vgname*/*lvname*, or @ *tag* set in the metadata of volume groups and logical volumes. A volume group or logical volume is activated only if a metadata tag matches. The default if there is no match, is not to activate.

If volume_list is not present and tags are defined on the host, then it activates the volume group or logical volumes only if a host tag matches a metadata tag.

If volume_list is defined, but empty, and no tags are defined on the host, then it does not activate.

If volume_list is undefined, it imposes no limits on LV activation (all are allowed).

4.9.4.4　Defining Activation in Multiple Host Name Configuration Files

You can use the activation code in a host's configuration file (`/etc/lvm/lvm_<host_tag>.conf`) when host tags are enabled in the `lvm.conf` file. For example, a server has two configuration files in the `/etc/lvm/` directory:

`lvm.conf`

`lvm_<host_tag>.conf`

At start-up, load the `/etc/lvm/lvm.conf` file, and process any tag settings in the file. If any host tags were defined, it loads the related `/etc/lvm/lvm_<host_tag>.conf` file. When it searches for a specific configuration file entry, it searches the host tag file first, then the `lvm.conf` file, and stops at the first match. Within the `lvm_<host_tag>.conf` file, use the reverse order that tags were set in. This allows the file for the last tag set to be searched first. New tags set in the host tag file will trigger additional configuration file loads.

4.9.5　Using Tags for a Simple Activation Control in a Cluster

You can set up a simple host name activation control by enabling the `hostname_tags` option in the `/etc/lvm/lvm.conf` file. Use the same file on every machine in a cluster so that it is a global setting.

1. In a text editor, add the following code to the `/etc/lvm/lvm.conf` file:

```
tags {
    hostname_tags = 1
}
```

2. Replicate the file to all hosts in the cluster.

3. From any machine in the cluster, add `db1` to the list of machines that activate `vg1/lvol2`:

```
sudo lvchange --addtag @db1 vg1/lvol2
```

4. On the `db1` server, enter the following to activate it:

```
sudo lvchange -ay vg1/vol2
```

4.9.6 Using Tags to Activate On Preferred Hosts in a Cluster

The examples in this section demonstrate two methods to accomplish the following:

- Activate volume group vg1 only on the database hosts db1 and db2.

- Activate volume group vg2 only on the file server host fs1.

- Activate nothing initially on the file server backup host fsb1, but be prepared for it to take over from the file server host fs1.

4.9.6.1 Option 1: Centralized Admin and Static Configuration Replicated Between Hosts

In the following solution, the single configuration file is replicated among multiple hosts.

1. Add the @database tag to the metadata of volume group vg1. In a terminal console, enter

   ```
   sudo vgchange --addtag @database vg1
   ```

2. Add the @fileserver tag to the metadata of volume group vg2. In a terminal console, enter

   ```
   sudo vgchange --addtag @fileserver vg2
   ```

3. In a text editor, modify the /etc/lvm/lvm.conf file with the following code to define the @database, @fileserver, @fileserverbackup tags.

   ```
   tags {
      database {
         host_list = [ "db1", "db2" ]
      }
      fileserver {
         host_list = [ "fs1" ]
      }
      fileserverbackup {
         host_list = [ "fsb1" ]
      }
   ```

```
}

activation {
    # Activate only if host has a tag that matches a metadata tag
    volume_list = [ "@*" ]
}
```

4. Replicate the modified /etc/lvm/lvm.conf file to the four hosts: db1, db2, fs1, and fsb1.

5. If the file server host goes down, vg2 can be brought up on fsb1 by entering the following commands in a terminal console on any node:

```
sudo vgchange --addtag @fileserverbackup vg2
sudo vgchange -ay vg2
```

4.9.6.2   Option 2: Localized Admin and Configuration

In the following solution, each host holds locally the information about which classes of volume to activate.

1. Add the @database tag to the metadata of volume group vg1. In a terminal console, enter

```
sudo vgchange --addtag @database vg1
```

2. Add the @fileserver tag to the metadata of volume group vg2. In a terminal console, enter

```
sudo vgchange --addtag @fileserver vg2
```

3. Enable host tags in the /etc/lvm/lvm.conf file:

   a. In a text editor, modify the /etc/lvm/lvm.conf file with the following code to enable host tag configuration files.

```
tags {
    hosttags = 1
```

```
}
```

b. Replicate the modified `/etc/lvm/lvm.conf` file to the four hosts: `db1`, `db2`, `fs1`, and `fsb1`.

4. On host `db1`, create an activation configuration file for the database host `db1`. In a text editor, create `/etc/lvm/lvm_db1.conf` file and add the following code:

```
activation {
    volume_list = [ "@database" ]
}
```

5. On host `db2`, create an activation configuration file for the database host `db2`. In a text editor, create `/etc/lvm/lvm_db2.conf` file and add the following code:

```
activation {
    volume_list = [ "@database" ]
}
```

6. On host fs1, create an activation configuration file for the file server host `fs1`. In a text editor, create `/etc/lvm/lvm_fs1.conf` file and add the following code:

```
activation {
    volume_list = [ "@fileserver" ]
}
```

7. If the file server host `fs1` goes down, to bring up a spare file server host fsb1 as a file server:

a. On host `fsb1`, create an activation configuration file for the host `fsb1`. In a text editor, create `/etc/lvm/lvm_fsb1.conf` file and add the following code:

```
activation {
    volume_list = [ "@fileserver" ]
}
```

b. In a terminal console, enter one of the following commands:

```
sudo vgchange -ay vg2
```

```
sudo vgchange -ay @fileserver
```

5 LVM Volume Snapshots

A Logical Volume Manager (LVM) logical volume snapshot is a copy-on-write technology that monitors changes to an existing volume's data blocks so that when a write is made to one of the blocks, the block's value at the snapshot time is copied to a snapshot volume. In this way, a point-in-time copy of the data is preserved until the snapshot volume is deleted.

5.1 Understanding Volume Snapshots

A file system snapshot contains metadata about itself and data blocks from a source logical volume that has changed since the snapshot was taken. When you access data via the snapshot, you see a point-in-time copy of the source logical volume. There is no need to restore data from backup media or to overwrite the changed data.

 Important: Mounting Volumes with Snapshots

During the snapshot's lifetime, the snapshot must be mounted before its source logical volume can be mounted.

LVM volume snapshots allow you to create a backup from a point-in-time view of the file system. The snapshot is created instantly and persists until you delete it. You can back up the file system from the snapshot while the volume itself continues to be available for users. The snapshot initially contains some metadata about the snapshot, but no actual data from the source logical volume. Snapshot uses copy-on-write technology to detect when data changes in an original data block. It copies the value it held when the snapshot was taken to a block in the snapshot volume, then allows the new data to be stored in the source block. As more blocks change from their original value on the source logical volume, the snapshot size grows.

When you are sizing the snapshot, consider how much data is expected to change on the source logical volume and how long you plan to keep the snapshot. The amount of space that you allocate for a snapshot volume can vary, depending on the size of the source logical volume, how long you plan to keep the snapshot, and the number of data blocks that are expected to change during the snapshot's lifetime. The snapshot volume cannot be resized after it is created. As a guide, create a snapshot volume that is about 10% of the size of the original logical volume. If you anticipate that every block in the source logical volume will change at least one time before you delete the snapshot, then the snapshot volume should be at least as large as the source logical volume plus some additional space for metadata about the snapshot volume. Less space is required if the data changes infrequently or if the expected lifetime is sufficiently brief.

In LVM2, snapshots are read/write by default. When you write data directly to the snapshot, that block is marked in the exception table as used, and never gets copied from the source logical volume. You can mount the snapshot volume, and test application changes by writing data directly to the snapshot volume. You can easily discard the changes by dismounting the snapshot, removing the snapshot, and then remounting the source logical volume.

In a virtual guest environment, you can use the snapshot function for LVM logical volumes you create on the server's disks, as you would on a physical server.

In a virtual host environment, you can use the snapshot function to back up the virtual machine's storage back-end, or to test changes to a virtual machine image, such as for patches or upgrades, without modifying the source logical volume. The virtual machine must be using an LVM logical volume as its storage back-end, as opposed to using a virtual disk file. You can mount the LVM logical volume and use it to store the virtual machine image as a file-backed disk, or you can assign the LVM logical volume as a physical disk to write to it as a block device.

Beginning in SLES 11 SP3, an LVM logical volume snapshot can be thinly provisioned. Thin provisioning is assumed if you create a snapshot without a specified size. The snapshot is created as a thin volume that uses space as needed from a thin pool. A thin snapshot volume has the same characteristics as any other thin volume. You can independently activate the volume, extend the volume, rename the volume, remove the volume, and even snapshot the volume.

 Important: Thinly Provisioned Volumes in a Cluster

To use thinly provisioned snapshots in a cluster, the source logical volume and its snapshots must be managed in a single cluster resource. This allows the volume and its snapshots to always be mounted exclusively on the same node.

When you are done with the snapshot, it is important to remove it from the system. A snapshot eventually fills up completely as data blocks change on the source logical volume. When the snapshot is full, it is disabled, which prevents you from remounting the source logical volume.

If you create multiple snapshots for a source logical volume, remove the snapshots in a last created, first deleted order.

5.2 Creating Linux Snapshots with LVM

The Logical Volume Manager (LVM) can be used for creating snapshots of your file system.
Open a terminal console and enter

```
sudo lvcreate -s [-L <size>] -n snap_volume source_volume_path
```

If no size is specified, the snapshot is created as a thin snapshot.
For example:

```
sudo lvcreate -s -L 1G -n linux01-snap /dev/lvm/linux01
```

The snapshot is created as the /dev/lvm/linux01-snap volume.

5.3 Monitoring a Snapshot

Open a terminal console and enter

```
sudo lvdisplay snap_volume
```

For example:

```
tux > sudo lvdisplay /dev/vg01/linux01-snap

--- Logical volume ---
  LV Name                /dev/lvm/linux01
  VG Name                vg01
  LV UUID                QHVJYh-PR3s-A4SG-s4Aa-MyWN-Ra7a-HL47KL
  LV Write Access        read/write
  LV snapshot status     active destination for /dev/lvm/linux01
  LV Status              available
  # open                 0
  LV Size                80.00 GB
  Current LE             1024
  COW-table size         8.00 GB
  COW-table LE           512
```

```
Allocated to snapshot   30%

Snapshot chunk size     8.00 KB

Segments                1

Allocation              inherit

Read ahead sectors      0

Block device            254:5
```

5.4   Deleting Linux Snapshots

Open a terminal console and enter

```
sudo lvremove snap_volume_path
```

For example:

```
sudo lvremove /dev/lvmvg/linux01-snap
```

5.5   Using Snapshots for Virtual Machines on a Virtual Host

Using an LVM logical volume for a virtual machine's back-end storage allows flexibility in administering the underlying device, such as making it easier to move storage objects, create snapshots, and back up data. You can mount the LVM logical volume and use it to store the virtual machine image as a file-backed disk, or you can assign the LVM logical volume as a physical disk to write to it as a block device. You can create a virtual disk image on the LVM logical volume, then snapshot the LVM.

You can leverage the read/write capability of the snapshot to create different instances of a virtual machine, where the changes are made to the snapshot for a particular virtual machine instance. You can create a virtual disk image on an LVM logical volume, snapshot the source logical volume, and modify the snapshot for a particular virtual machine instance. You can create another snapshot of the source logical volume, and modify it for a different virtual machine instance. The majority of the data for the different virtual machine instances resides with the image on the source logical volume.

You can also leverage the read/write capability of the snapshot to preserve the virtual disk image while testing patches or upgrades in the guest environment. You create a snapshot of the LVM volume that contains the image, and then run the virtual machine on the snapshot location. The source logical volume is unchanged, and all changes for that machine are written to the snapshot. To return to the source logical volume of the virtual machine image, you power off the virtual machine, then remove the snapshot from the source logical volume. To start over, you re-create the snapshot, mount the snapshot, and restart the virtual machine on the snapshot image.

The following procedure uses a file-backed virtual disk image and the Xen hypervisor. You can adapt the procedure in this section for other hypervisors that run on the SUSE Linux platform, such as KVM. To run a file-backed virtual machine image from the snapshot volume:

1. Ensure that the source logical volume that contains the file-backed virtual machine image is mounted, such as at mount point /var/lib/xen/images/<image_name>.

2. Create a snapshot of the LVM logical volume with enough space to store the differences that you expect.

   ```
   sudo lvcreate -s -L 20G -n myvm-snap /dev/lvmvg/myvm
   ```

   If no size is specified, the snapshot is created as a thin snapshot.

3. Create a mount point where you will mount the snapshot volume.

   ```
   sudo mkdir -p /mnt/xen/vm/myvm-snap
   ```

4. Mount the snapshot volume at the mount point you created.

   ```
   sudo mount -t auto /dev/lvmvg/myvm-snap /mnt/xen/vm/myvm-snap
   ```

5. In a text editor, copy the configuration file for the source virtual machine, modify the paths to point to the file-backed image file on the mounted snapshot volume, and save the file such as /etc/xen/myvm-snap.cfg.

6. Start the virtual machine using the mounted snapshot volume of the virtual machine.

   ```
   sudo xm create -c /etc/xen/myvm-snap.cfg
   ```

7. (Optional) Remove the snapshot, and use the unchanged virtual machine image on the source logical volume.

```
sudo unmount /mnt/xenvms/myvm-snap
sudo lvremove -f /dev/lvmvg/mylvm-snap
```

8. (Optional) Repeat this process as desired.

5.6   Merging a Snapshot with the Source Logical Volume to Revert Changes or Roll Back to a Previous State

Snapshots can be useful if you need to roll back or restore data on a volume to a previous state. For example, you might need to revert data changes that resulted from an administrator error or a failed or undesirable package installation or upgrade.

You can use the `lvconvert --merge` command to revert the changes made to an LVM logical volume. The merging begins as follows:

- If both the source logical volume and snapshot volume are not open, the merge begins immediately.

- If the source logical volume or snapshot volume are open, the merge starts the first time either the source logical volume or snapshot volume are activated and both are closed.

- If the source logical volume cannot be closed, such as the root file system, the merge is deferred until the next time the server reboots and the source logical volume is activated.

- If the source logical volume contains a virtual machine image, you must shut down the virtual machine, deactivate the source logical volume and snapshot volume (by dismounting them in that order), and then issue the merge command. Because the source logical volume is automatically remounted and the snapshot volume is deleted when the merge is complete, you should not restart the virtual machine until after the merge is complete. After the merge is complete, you use the resulting logical volume for the virtual machine.

After a merge begins, the merge continues automatically after server restarts until it is complete. A new snapshot cannot be created for the source logical volume while a merge is in progress.

While the merge is in progress, reads or writes to the source logical volume are transparently redirected to the snapshot that is being merged. This allows users to immediately view and access the data as it was when the snapshot was created. They do not need to wait for the merge to complete.

When the merge is complete, the source logical volume contains the same data as it did when the snapshot was taken, plus any data changes made after the merge began. The resulting logical volume has the source logical volume's name, minor number, and UUID. The source logical volume is automatically remounted, and the snapshot volume is removed.

1. Open a terminal console and enter

```
sudo lvconvert --merge  [-b] [-i seconds] [snap_volume_path[...snapN]|
@volume_tag]
```

You can specify one or multiple snapshots on the command line. You can alternatively tag multiple source logical volumes with the same volume tag then specify @<volume_tag> on the command line. The snapshots for the tagged volumes are merged to their respective source logical volumes. For information about tagging logical volumes, see Section 4.9, "Tagging LVM2 Storage Objects".
The options include:

-b,
--background

   Run the daemon in the background. This allows multiple specified snapshots to be merged concurrently in parallel.

-i,
--interval < seconds >

   Report progress as a percentage at regular intervals. Specify the interval in seconds.

For more information about this command, see the **lvconvert(8)** man page.
For example:

```
sudo lvconvert --merge /dev/lvmvg/linux01-snap
```

This command merges /dev/lvmvg/linux01-snap into its source logical volume.

Merging a Snapshot with the Source Logical Volume to Revert Changes or Roll Back to a Previous State

```
sudo lvconvert --merge @mytag
```

If `lvol1`, `lvol2`, and `lvol3` are all tagged with `mytag`, each snapshot volume is merged serially with its respective source logical volume; that is: `lvol1`, then `lvol2`, then `lvol3`. If the `--background` option is specified, the snapshots for the respective tagged logical volume are merged concurrently in parallel.

2. (Optional) If both the source logical volume and snapshot volume are open and they can be closed, you can manually deactivate and activate the source logical volume to get the merge to start immediately.

```
sudo umount original_volume
sudo lvchange -an original_volume
sudo lvchange -ay original_volume
sudo mount original_volume mount_point
```

For example:

```
sudo umount /dev/lvmvg/lvol01
sudo lvchange -an /dev/lvmvg/lvol01
sudo lvchange -ay /dev/lvmvg/lvol01
sudo mount /dev/lvmvg/lvol01 /mnt/lvol01
```

3. (Optional) If both the source logical volume and snapshot volume are open and the source logical volume cannot be closed, such as the `root` file system, you can restart the server and mount the source logical volume to get the merge to start immediately after the restart.

III Software RAID

6 Software RAID Configuration

The purpose of RAID (redundant array of independent disks) is to combine several hard disk partitions into one large virtual hard disk to optimize performance, data security, or both. Most RAID controllers use the SCSI protocol because it can address a larger number of hard disks in a more effective way than the IDE protocol and is more suitable for parallel processing of commands. There are some RAID controllers that support IDE or SATA hard disks. Software RAID provides the advantages of RAID systems without the additional cost of hardware RAID controllers. However, this requires some CPU time and has memory requirements that make it unsuitable for real high performance computers.

> ⓘ **Important: No RAID on Cluster File Systems**
>
> Software RAID is not supported underneath clustered file systems such as OCFS2, because RAID does not support concurrent activation. If you want RAID for OCFS2, you need the RAID to be handled by the storage subsystem.

SUSE Linux Enterprise offers the option of combining several hard disks into one soft RAID system. RAID implies several strategies for combining several hard disks in a RAID system, each with different goals, advantages, and characteristics. These variations are commonly known as *RAID levels*.

6.1 Understanding RAID Levels

This section describes common RAID levels 0, 1, 2, 3, 4, 5, and nested RAID levels.

6.1.1 RAID 0

This level improves the performance of your data access by spreading out blocks of each file across multiple disks. Actually, this is not really a RAID, because it does not provide data backup, but the name *RAID 0* for this type of system has become the norm. With RAID 0, two or more hard disks are pooled together. The performance is very good, but the RAID system is destroyed and your data lost if even one hard disk fails.

6.1.2   RAID 1

This level provides adequate security for your data, because the data is copied to another hard disk 1:1. This is known as *hard disk mirroring.* If a disk is destroyed, a copy of its contents is available on another mirrored disk. All disks except one could be damaged without endangering your data. However, if damage is not detected, damaged data might be mirrored to the correct disk and the data is corrupted that way. The writing performance suffers a little in the copying process compared to when using single disk access (10 to 20 percent slower), but read access is significantly faster in comparison to any one of the normal physical hard disks, because the data is duplicated so can be scanned in parallel. RAID 1 generally provides nearly twice the read transaction rate of single disks and almost the same write transaction rate as single disks.

6.1.3   RAID 2 and RAID 3

These are not typical RAID implementations. Level 2 stripes data at the bit level rather than the block level. Level 3 provides byte-level striping with a dedicated parity disk and cannot service simultaneous multiple requests. Both levels are rarely used.

6.1.4   RAID 4

Level 4 provides block-level striping like Level 0 combined with a dedicated parity disk. If a data disk fails, the parity data is used to create a replacement disk. However, the parity disk might create a bottleneck for write access. Nevertheless, Level 4 is sometimes used.

6.1.5   RAID 5

RAID 5 is an optimized compromise between Level 0 and Level 1 in terms of performance and redundancy. The hard disk space equals the number of disks used minus one. The data is distributed over the hard disks as with RAID 0. *Parity blocks,* created on one of the partitions, are there for security reasons. They are linked to each other with XOR, enabling the contents to be reconstructed by the corresponding parity block in case of system failure. With RAID 5, no more than one hard disk can fail at the same time. If one hard disk fails, it must be replaced as soon as possible to avoid the risk of losing data.

6.1.6 RAID 6

RAID 6 is essentially an extension of RAID 5 that allows for additional fault tolerance by using a second independent distributed parity scheme (dual parity). Even if two of the hard disks fail during the data recovery process, the system continues to be operational, with no data loss.

RAID 6 provides for extremely high data fault tolerance by sustaining multiple simultaneous drive failures. It handles the loss of any two devices without data loss. Accordingly, it requires $N + 2$ drives to store N drives worth of data. It requires a minimum of four devices.

The performance for RAID 6 is slightly lower but comparable to RAID 5 in normal mode and single disk failure mode. It is very slow in dual disk failure mode. A RAID 6 configuration needs a considerable amount of CPU time and memory for write operations.

TABLE 6.1: COMPARISON OF RAID 5 AND RAID 6

Feature	RAID 5	RAID 6
Number of devices	$N + 1$, minimum of 3	$N + 2$, minimum of 4
Parity	Distributed, single	Distributed, dual
Performance	Medium impact on write and rebuild	More impact on sequential write than RAID 5
Fault-tolerance	Failure of one component device	Failure of two component devices

6.1.7 Nested and Complex RAID Levels

Several other RAID levels have been developed, such as RAIDn, RAID 10, RAID 0 + 1, RAID 30, and RAID 50. Some are proprietary implementations created by hardware vendors. Examples for creating RAID 10 configurations can be found in *Chapter 8, Creating Software RAID 10 Devices*.

6.2 Soft RAID Configuration with YaST

The YaST soft RAID configuration can be reached from the YaST Expert Partitioner. This partitioning tool also enables you to edit and delete existing partitions and create new ones that should be used with soft RAID. These instructions apply on setting up RAID levels 0, 1, 5, and 6. Setting up RAID 10 configurations is explained in *Chapter 8, Creating Software RAID 10 Devices*.

1. Launch YaST and open the *Partitioner*.

2. If necessary, create partitions that should be used with your RAID configuration. Do not format them and set the partition type to *0xFD Linux RAID*. When using existing partitions it is not necessary to change their partition type—YaST will automatically do so. Refer to *Book "Deployment Guide", Chapter 14 "Advanced Disk Setup", Section 14.1 "Using the YaST Partitioner"* for details.

   It is strongly recommended to use partitions stored on different hard disks to decrease the risk of losing data if one is defective (RAID 1 and 5) and to optimize the performance of RAID 0.

   For RAID 0 at least two partitions are needed. RAID 1 requires exactly two partitions, while at least three partitions are required for RAID 5. A RAID 6 setup requires at least four partitions. It is recommended to use only partitions of the same size because each segment can contribute only the same amount of space as the smallest sized partition.

3. In the left panel, select *RAID*.

   A list of existing RAID configurations opens in the right panel.

4. At the lower left of the RAID page, click *Add RAID*.

5. Select a *RAID Type* and *Add* an appropriate number of partitions from the *Available Devices* dialog.

You can optionally assign a *RAID Name* to your RAID. It will make it available as `/dev/md/name`. See *Section 6.2.1, "RAID Names"* for more information.

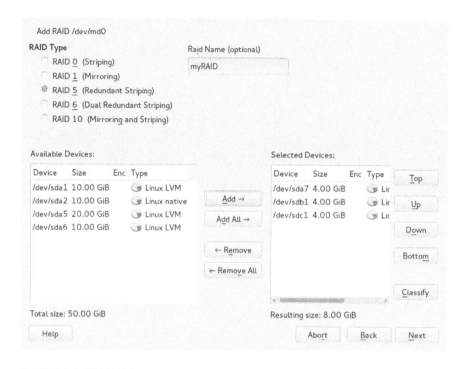

FIGURE 6.1: EXAMPLE RAID 5 CONFIGURATION

Proceed with *Next*.

6. Select the *Chunk Size* and, if applicable, the *Parity Algorithm*. The optimal chunk size depends on the type of data and the type of RAID. See https://raid.wiki.kernel.org/index.php/RAID_setup#Chunk_sizes for more information. More information on parity algorithms can be found with `man 8 mdadm` when searching for the `--layout` option. If unsure, stick with the defaults.

7. Choose a *Role* for the volume. Your choice here only affects the default values for the upcoming dialog. They can be changed in the next step. If in doubt, choose *Raw Volume (Unformatted)*.

8. Under *Formatting Options*, select *Format Partition*, then select the *File system*. The content of the *Options* menu depends on the file system. Usually there is no need to change the defaults.
Under *Mounting Options*, select *Mount partition*, then select the mount point. Click *Fstab Options* to add special mounting options for the volume.

9. Click *Finish*.

10. Click *Next*, verify that the changes are listed, then click *Finish*.

6.2.1 RAID Names

By default, software RAID devices have numeric names following the pattern `mdN`, where `N` is a number. As such they can be accessed as, for example, `/dev/md127` and are listed as `md127` in `/proc/mdstat` and `/proc/partitions`. Working with these names can be clumsy. SUSE Linux Enterprise Server offers two ways to work around this problem:

Providing a Named Link to the Device

You can optionally specify a name for the RAID device when creating it with YaST or on the command line with **mdadm --create '/dev/md/** *name*'. The device name will still be `mdN`, but a link `/dev/md/`*name* will be created:

```
tux > ls -og /dev/md
total 0
lrwxrwxrwx 1 8 Dec  9 15:11 myRAID -> ../md127
```

The device will still be listed as `md127` under `/proc`.

Providing a Named Device

In case a named link to the device is not sufficient for your setup, add the line CREATE names = yes to `/etc/mdadm.conf` by running the following command:

```
sudo echo "CREATE names=yes" >> /etc/mdadm.conf
```

It will cause names like `myRAID` to be used as a "real" device name. The device will not only be accessible at `/dev/myRAID`, but also be listed as `myRAID` under `/proc`. Note that this will only apply to RAIDs configured after the change to the configuration file. Active RAIDS will continue to use the `mdN` names until they get stopped and re-assembled.

 Warning: Incompatible Tools

> Not all tools may support named RAID devices. In case a tool expects a RAID device to be named `mdN`, it will fail to identify the devices.

6.3 Troubleshooting Software RAIDs

Check the `/proc/mdstat` file to find out whether a RAID partition has been damaged. If a disk fails, shut down your Linux system and replace the defective hard disk with a new one partitioned the same way. Then restart your system and enter the command **mdadm /dev/mdX --add /dev/sdX**. Replace X with your particular device identifiers. This integrates the hard disk automatically into the RAID system and fully reconstructs it (for all RAID levels except for RAID 0).

Although you can access all data during the rebuild, you might encounter some performance issues until the RAID has been fully rebuilt.

6.3.1 Recovery after Failing Disk is Back Again

There are several reasons a disk included in a RAID array may fail. Here is a list of the most common ones:

- Problems with the disk media.

- Disk drive controller failure.

- Broken connection to the disk.

In the case of the disk media or controller failure, the device needs to be replaced or repaired. If a hot-spare was not configured within the RAID, then manual intervention is required.

In the last case, the failed device can be automatically re-added by the **mdadm** command after the connection is repaired (which might be automatic).

Because **md** / **mdadm** cannot reliably determine what caused the disk failure, it assumes a serious disk error and treats any failed device as faulty until it is explicitly told that the device is reliable.

Under some circumstances—such as storage devices with the internal RAID array— the connection problems are very often the cause of the device failure. In such case, you can tell **mdadm** that it is safe to automatically `--re-add` the device after it appears. You can do this by adding the following line to `/etc/mdadm.conf`:

```
POLICY action=re-add
```

Note that the device will be automatically re-added after re-appearing only if the udev rules cause **mdadm -I** *disk_device_name* to be run on any device that spontaneously appears (default behavior), and if write-intent bitmaps are configured (they are by default).

If you want this policy to only apply to some devices and not to the others, then the `path=` option can be added to the `POLICY` line in `/etc/mdadm.conf` to restrict the non-default action to only selected devices. Wild cards can be used to identify groups of devices. See **man 5 mdadm.conf** for more information.

6.4   For More Information

Configuration instructions and more details for soft RAID can be found in the HOWTOs at:

- *The Linux RAID wiki*: https://raid.wiki.kernel.org/index.php/Linux_Raid

- *The Software RAID HOWTO* in the `/usr/share/doc/packages/mdadm/Software-RAID.HOWTO.html` file

Linux RAID mailing lists are also available, such as *linux-raid* at http://marc.info/?l=linux-raid.

7   Configuring Software RAID 1 for the Root Partition

In SUSE Linux Enterprise Server, the Device Mapper RAID tool has been integrated into the YaST Partitioner. You can use the partitioner at install time to create a software RAID 1 for the system device that contains your root (/) partition. The /boot partition cannot be stored on a RAID partition unless it is RAID 1. In this case the boot loader must be installed in MBR.

7.1   Prerequisites for Using a Software RAID 1 Device for the Root Partition

Ensure that your configuration meets the following requirements:

* You need two hard disks to create the RAID 1 mirror device. The hard disks should be similarly sized. The RAID assumes the size of the smaller drive. The block storage devices can be any combination of local (in or directly attached to the machine), Fibre Channel storage subsystems, or iSCSI storage subsystems.

* A separate partition for /boot is not required if you install the boot loader in the MBR. If installing the boot loader in the MBR is not an option, /boot needs to reside on a separate partition that is not part of a software RAID.

* If you are using hardware RAID devices, do not attempt to run software RAIDs on top of it.

* If you are using iSCSI target devices, you must enable the iSCSI initiator support before you create the RAID device.

* If your storage subsystem provides multiple I/O paths between the server and its directly attached local devices, Fibre Channel devices, or iSCSI devices that you want to use in the software RAID, you must enable the multipath support before you create the RAID device.

7.2   Setting up the System with a Software RAID 1 Device for the Root (/) Partition

1. Start the installation with YaST and proceed as described in *Book "Deployment Guide",* *Chapter 6 "Installation with YaST"* until you reach the *Suggested Partitioning* step.

2. Click *Expert Partitioner* to open the custom partitioning tool.

3. (Optional) If there are iSCSI target devices that you want to use, you need to enable the iSCSI Initiator software by choosing *Configure* › *Configure iSCSI* from the lower right section of the screen. Refer to *Chapter 13, Mass Storage over IP Networks: iSCSI* for further details.

4. (Optional) If there are multiple I/O paths to the devices that you want to use you need to enable multipath support by choosing *Configure* › *Configure Multipath* › *Yes* from the lower right section of the screen.

5. (Optional) In case you have neither configured iSCSI or Multipath, the default proposal settings are shown. Click *Rescan Devices* to delete them.

6. Set up the *0xFD Linux RAID* format for each of the devices you want to use for the software RAID 1.

   a. In the left panel, select *Hard Disks* and select the device you want to use, then click *Add Partition*.

   b. Under *New Partition Type*, select *Primary Partition*, then click *Next*.

   c. Under *New Partition Size*, specify the size to use, then click *Next*.

   d. Under *Role*, choose *Raw Volume (unformatted)*.

   e. Select *Do not format* and set the *File SystemID* to *0xFD Linux RAID*.

   f. Click *Finish* and repeat these instructions for the second partition.

7. Create the RAID device.

  a. In the left panel, select *RAID* and then *Add RAID*.

  b. Set the *RAID Type* to *RAID 1 (Mirroring)* and the *RAID name* to `system`.

  c. Select the two RAID devices you prepared in the previous step from the *Available Devices* section and *Add* them.

Setting up the System with a Software RAID 1 Device for the Root (/) Partition

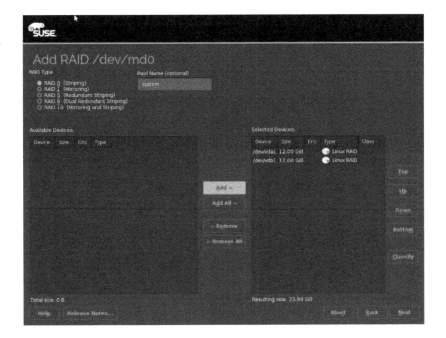

Proceed with *Next*.

d. Under *RAID Options*, select the chunk size from the drop-down box. The chunk size does not have many performance implications for RAID 1, so sticking with the default is recommended.

e. Under *Role*, select *Operating System*.

f. Leave this dialog with *Finish*.

8. The software RAID device is managed by Device Mapper, and creates a device under the `/dev/md/system` path. Click *Accept* to leave the partitioner.
   The new proposal appears on the *Suggested Partitioning* page.

9. Continue with the installation.
   Whenever you reboot your server, Device Mapper is started at boot time so that the software RAID is automatically recognized, and the operating system on the root (/) partition can be started.

8 Creating Software RAID 10 Devices

This section describes how to set up nested and complex RAID 10 devices. A RAID 10 device consists of nested RAID 1 (mirroring) and RAID 0 (striping) arrays. Nested RAIDs can either be set up as striped mirrors (RAID 1 + 0) or as mirrored stripes (RAID 0 + 1). A complex RAID 10 setup also combines mirrors and stripes and additional data security by supporting a higher data redundancy level.

8.1 Creating Nested RAID 10 Devices with mdadm

A nested RAID device consists of a RAID array that uses another RAID array as its basic element, instead of using physical disks. The goal of this configuration is to improve the performance and fault tolerance of the RAID. Setting up nested RAID levels is not supported by YaST, but can be done by using the mdadm command line tool.

Based on the order of nesting, two different nested RAIDs can be set up. This document uses the following terminology:

- **RAID 1+0:** RAID 1 (mirror) arrays are built first, then combined to form a RAID 0 (stripe) array.

- **RAID 0+1:** RAID 0 (stripe) arrays are built first, then combined to form a RAID 1 (mirror) array.

The following table describes the advantages and disadvantages of RAID 10 nesting as 1 + 0 versus 0 + 1. It assumes that the storage objects you use reside on different disks, each with a dedicated I/O capability.

TABLE 8.1: NESTED RAID LEVELS

RAID Level	Description	Performance and Fault Tolerance
10 (1 + 0)	RAID 0 (stripe) built with RAID 1 (mirror) arrays	RAID 1 + 0 provides high levels of I/O performance, data redundancy, and disk fault tolerance. Because each member device in the RAID 0 is mirrored individually, multiple disk failures can be tolerated and data remains available as long as the disks that fail are in different mirrors.

RAID Level	Description	Performance and Fault Tolerance
		You can optionally configure a spare for each underlying mirrored array, or configure a spare to serve a spare group that serves all mirrors.
10 (0 + 1)	RAID 1 (mirror) built with RAID 0 (stripe) arrays	RAID 0 + 1 provides high levels of I/O performance and data redundancy, but slightly less fault tolerance than a 1 + 0. If multiple disks fail on one side of the mirror, then the other mirror is available. However, if disks are lost concurrently on both sides of the mirror, all data is lost.

This solution offers less disk fault tolerance than a 1 + 0 solution, but if you need to perform maintenance or maintain the mirror on a different site, you can take an entire side of the mirror offline and still have a fully functional storage device. Also, if you lose the connection between the two sites, either site operates independently of the other. That is not true if you stripe the mirrored segments, because the mirrors are managed at a lower level.

If a device fails, the mirror on that side fails because RAID 1 is not fault-tolerant. Create a new RAID 0 to replace the failed side, then resynchronize the mirrors. |

8.1.1   Creating Nested RAID 10 (1+0) with mdadm

A nested RAID 1 + 0 is built by creating two or more RAID 1 (mirror) devices, then using them as component devices in a RAID 0.

! Important: Multipathing

If you need to manage multiple connections to the devices, you must configure multipath I/O before configuring the RAID devices. For information, see *Chapter 15, Managing Multipath I/O for Devices*.

The procedure in this section uses the device names shown in the following table. Ensure that you modify the device names with the names of your own devices.

TABLE 8.2: SCENARIO FOR CREATING A RAID 10 (1+0) BY NESTING

Raw Devices	RAID 1 (mirror)	RAID 1 + 0 (striped mirrors)
/dev/sdb1 /dev/sdc1	/dev/md0	/dev/md2
/dev/sdd1 /dev/sde1	/dev/md1	

1. Open a terminal console.

2. If necessary, create four 0xFD Linux RAID partitions of equal size using a disk partitioner such as parted.

3. Create two software RAID 1 devices, using two different devices for each device. At the command prompt, enter these two commands:

```
sudo mdadm --create /dev/md0 --run --level=1 --raid-devices=2 /dev/sdb1 /dev/
sdc1
sudo mdadm --create /dev/md1 --run --level=1 --raid-devices=2 /dev/sdd1 /dev/
sde1
```

4. Create the nested RAID 1 + 0 device. At the command prompt, enter the following command using the software RAID 1 devices you created in the previous step:

```
sudo mdadm --create /dev/md2 --run --level=0 --chunk=64 \
--raid-devices=2 /dev/md0 /dev/md1
```

The default chunk size is 64 KB.

5. Create a file system on the RAID $1+0$ device /dev/md2, for example an XFS file system:

```
sudo mkfs.xfs /dev/md2
```

Modify the command if you want to use a different file system.

6. Edit the /etc/mdadm.conf file or create it, if it does not exist (for example by running **sudo vi /etc/mdadm.conf**). Add the following lines (if the file already exists, the first line probably already exists).

```
DEVICE containers partitions
ARRAY /dev/md0 UUID=UUID
ARRAY /dev/md1 UUID=UUID
ARRAY /dev/md2 UUID=UUID
```

The UUID of each device can be retrieved with the following command:

```
sudo mdadm -D /dev/DEVICE | grep UUID
```

7. Edit the /etc/fstab file to add an entry for the RAID $1+0$ device /dev/md2. The following example shows an entry for a RAID device with the XFS file system and /data as a mount point.

```
/dev/md2 /data xfs defaults 1 2
```

8. Mount the RAID device:

```
sudo mount /data
```

8.1.2 Creating Nested RAID 10 (0+1) with mdadm

A nested RAID $0+1$ is built by creating two to four RAID 0 (striping) devices, then mirroring them as component devices in a RAID 1.

Important: Multipathing

If you need to manage multiple connections to the devices, you must configure multipath I/O before configuring the RAID devices. For information, see *Chapter 15, Managing Multipath I/O for Devices*.

In this configuration, spare devices cannot be specified for the underlying RAID 0 devices because RAID 0 cannot tolerate a device loss. If a device fails on one side of the mirror, you must create a replacement RAID 0 device, than add it into the mirror.

The procedure in this section uses the device names shown in the following table. Ensure that you modify the device names with the names of your own devices.

TABLE 8.3: SCENARIO FOR CREATING A RAID 10 (0+1) BY NESTING

Raw Devices	RAID 0 (stripe)	RAID 0 + 1 (mirrored stripes)
/dev/sdb1 /dev/sdc1	/dev/md0	/dev/md2
/dev/sdd1 /dev/sde1	/dev/md1	

1. Open a terminal console.

2. If necessary, create four 0xFD Linux RAID partitions of equal size using a disk partitioner such as parted.

3. Create two software RAID 0 devices, using two different devices for each RAID 0 device. At the command prompt, enter these two commands:

```
sudo mdadm --create /dev/md0 --run --level=0 --chunk=64 \
--raid-devices=2 /dev/sdb1 /dev/sdc1
sudo mdadm --create /dev/md1 --run --level=0 --chunk=64 \
--raid-devices=2 /dev/sdd1 /dev/sde1
```

The default chunk size is 64 KB.

4. Create the nested RAID 0 + 1 device. At the command prompt, enter the following command using the software RAID 0 devices you created in the previous step:

```
sudo mdadm --create /dev/md2 --run --level=1 --raid-devices=2 /dev/md0 /dev/md1
```

5. Create a file system on the RAID 1 + 0 device /dev/md2, for example an XFS file system:

```
sudo mkfs.xfs /dev/md2
```

Modify the command if you want to use a different file system.

6. Edit the /etc/mdadm.conf file or create it, if it does not exist (for example by running **sudo vi /etc/mdadm.conf**). Add the following lines (if the file exists, the first line probably already exists, too).

```
DEVICE containers partitions
ARRAY /dev/md0 UUID=UUID
ARRAY /dev/md1 UUID=UUID
ARRAY /dev/md2 UUID=UUID
```

The UUID of each device can be retrieved with the following command:

```
sudo mdadm -D /dev/DEVICE | grep UUID
```

7. Edit the /etc/fstab file to add an entry for the RAID 1 + 0 device /dev/md2. The following example shows an entry for a RAID device with the XFS file system and /data as a mount point.

```
/dev/md2 /data xfs defaults 1 2
```

8. Mount the RAID device:

```
sudo mount /data
```

8.2   Creating a Complex RAID 10

YaST (and **mdadm** with the --level=10 option) creates a single complex software RAID 10 that combines features of both RAID 0 (striping) and RAID 1 (mirroring). Multiple copies of all data blocks are arranged on multiple drives following a striping discipline. Component devices should be the same size.

The complex RAID 10 is similar in purpose to a nested RAID 10 (1 + 0), but differs in the following ways:

TABLE 8.4: COMPLEX VS. NESTED RAID 10

Feature	Complex RAID 10	Nested RAID 10 (1 + 0)
Number of devices	Allows an even or odd number of component devices	Requires an even number of component devices
Component devices	Managed as a single RAID device	Manage as a nested RAID device
Striping	Striping occurs in the near or far layout on component devices. The far layout provides sequential read throughput that scales by number of drives, rather than number of RAID 1 pairs.	Striping occurs consecutively across component devices
Multiple copies of data	Two or more copies, up to the number of devices in the array	Copies on each mirrored segment
Hot spare devices	A single spare can service all component devices	Configure a spare for each underlying mirrored array, or configure a spare to serve a spare group that serves all mirrors.

8.2.1   Number of Devices and Replicas in the Complex RAID 10

When configuring a complex RAID 10 array, you must specify the number of replicas of each data block that are required. The default number of replicas is two, but the value can be two to the number of devices in the array.

You must use at least as many component devices as the number of replicas you specify. However, the number of component devices in a RAID 10 array does not need to be a multiple of the number of replicas of each data block. The effective storage size is the number of devices divided by the number of replicas.

For example, if you specify two replicas for an array created with five component devices, a copy of each block is stored on two different devices. The effective storage size for one copy of all data is 5/2 or 2.5 times the size of a component device.

8.2.2 Layout

The complex RAID 10 setup supports three different layouts which define how the data blocks are arranged on the disks. The available layouts are near (default), far and offset. They have different performance characteristics, so it is important to choose the right layout for your workload.

8.2.2.1 Near Layout

With the near layout, copies of a block of data are striped near each other on different component devices. That is, multiple copies of one data block are at similar offsets in different devices. Near is the default layout for RAID 10. For example, if you use an odd number of component devices and two copies of data, some copies are perhaps one chunk further into the device.

The near layout for the complex RAID 10 yields read and write performance similar to RAID 0 over half the number of drives.

Near layout with an even number of disks and two replicas:

```
sda1 sdb1 sdc1 sde1
  0    0    1    1
  2    2    3    3
  4    4    5    5
  6    6    7    7
  8    8    9    9
```

Near layout with an odd number of disks and two replicas:

```
sda1 sdb1 sdc1 sde1 sdf1
```

```
 0   0   1   1   2
 2   3   3   4   4
 5   5   6   6   7
 7   8   8   9   9
10  10  11  11  12
```

8.2.2.2   Far Layout

The far layout stripes data over the early part of all drives, then stripes a second copy of the data over the later part of all drives, making sure that all copies of a block are on different drives. The second set of values starts halfway through the component drives.

With a far layout, the read performance of the complex RAID 10 is similar to a RAID 0 over the full number of drives, but write performance is substantially slower than a RAID 0 because there is more seeking of the drive heads. It is best used for read-intensive operations such as for read-only file servers.

The speed of the RAID 10 for writing is similar to other mirrored RAID types, like RAID 1 and RAID 10 using near layout, as the elevator of the file system schedules the writes in a more optimal way than raw writing. Using RAID 10 in the far layout is well suited for mirrored writing applications.

Far layout with an even number of disks and two replicas:

```
sda1 sdb1 sdc1 sde1
  0    1    2    3
  4    5    6    7
  .  .  .
  3    0    1    2
  7    4    5    6
```

Far layout with an odd number of disks and two replicas:

```
sda1 sdb1 sdc1 sde1 sdf1
  0    1    2    3    4
  5    6    7    8    9
  .  .  .
  4    0    1    2    3
```

```
 9    5    6    7    8
```

8.2.2.3 Offset Layout

The offset layout duplicates stripes so that the multiple copies of a given chunk are laid out on consecutive drives and at consecutive offsets. Effectively, each stripe is duplicated and the copies are offset by one device. This should give similar read characteristics to a far layout if a suitably large chunk size is used, but without as much seeking for writes.

Offset layout with an even number of disks and two replicas:

```
sda1 sdb1 sdc1 sde1
  0    1    2    3
  3    0    1    2
  4    5    6    7
  7    4    5    6
  8    9   10   11
 11    8    9   10
```

Offset layout with an odd number of disks and two replicas:

```
sda1 sdb1 sdc1 sde1 sdf1
  0    1    2    3    4
  4    0    1    2    3
  5    6    7    8    9
  9    5    6    7    8
 10   11   12   13   14
 14   10   11   12   13
```

8.2.2.4 Specifying the number of Replicas and the Layout with YaST and mdadm

The number of replicas and the layout is specified as *Parity Algorithm* in YaST or with the `--layout` parameter for mdadm. The following values are accepted:

`nN`

> Specify `n` for near layout and replace `N` with the number of replicas. `n2` is the default that is used when not configuring layout and the number of replicas.

`fN`

> Specify `f` for far layout and replace `N` with the number of replicas.

`oN`

> Specify `o` for offset layout and replace `N` with the number of replicas.

 Note: Number of Replicas

> YaST automatically offers a selection of all possible values for the *Parity Algorithm* parameter.

8.2.3 Creating a Complex RAID 10 with the YaST Partitioner

1. Launch YaST and open the Partitioner.

2. If necessary, create partitions that should be used with your RAID configuration. Do not format them and set the partition type to *0xFD Linux RAID*. When using existing partitions it is not necessary to change their partition type—YaST will automatically do so. Refer to *Book "Deployment Guide", Chapter 14 "Advanced Disk Setup", Section 14.1 "Using the YaST Partitioner"* for details.

   For RAID 10 at least four partitions are needed. It is strongly recommended to use partitions stored on different hard disks to decrease the risk of losing data if one is defective. It is recommended to use only partitions of the same size because each segment can contribute only the same amount of space as the smallest sized partition.

3. In the left panel, select *RAID*.

   A list of existing RAID configurations opens in the right panel.

4. At the lower left of the RAID page, click *Add RAID*.

5. Under *RAID Type*, select *RAID 10 (Mirroring and Striping)*.

   You can optionally assign a *RAID Name* to your RAID. It will make it available as /dev/ md/*name*. See *Section 6.2.1, "RAID Names"* for more information.

6. In the *Available Devices* list, select the desired partitions, then click *Add* to move them to the *Selected Devices* list.

7. (Optional) Click *Classify* to specify the preferred order of the disks in the RAID array.

   For RAID types such as RAID 10, where the order of added disks matters, you can specify the order in which the devices will be used. This will ensure that one half of the array resides on one disk subsystem and the other half of the array resides on a different disk subsystem. For example, if one disk subsystem fails, the system keeps running from the second disk subsystem.

   a. Select each disk in turn and click one of the *Class X* buttons, where X is the letter you want to assign to the disk. Available classes are A, B, C, D and E but for many cases fewer classes are needed (only A and B, for example). Assign all available RAID disks this way.

      You can press the Ctrl or Shift key to select multiple devices. You can also right-click a selected device and choose the appropriate class from the context menu.

   b. Specify the order of the devices by selecting one of the sorting options:

Sorted: Sorts all devices of class A before all devices of class B and so on. For example: AABBCC.

Interleaved: Sorts devices by the first device of class A, then first device of class B, then all the following classes with assigned devices. Then the second device of class A, the second device of class B, and so on follows. All devices without a class are sorted to the end of the devices list. For example: ABCABC.

Pattern File: Select an existing file that contains multiple lines, where each is a regular expression and a class name ("sda.* A"). All devices that match the regular expression are assigned to the specified class for that line. The regular expression is matched against the kernel name (/dev/sda1), the udev path name (/dev/disk/by-path/pci-0000:00:1f.2-scsi-0:0:0:0-part1) and then the udev ID (dev/disk/by-id/ata-ST3500418AS_9VMN8X8L-part1). The first match made determines the class if a device's name matches more than one regular expression.

  c. At the bottom of the dialog, click *OK* to confirm the order.

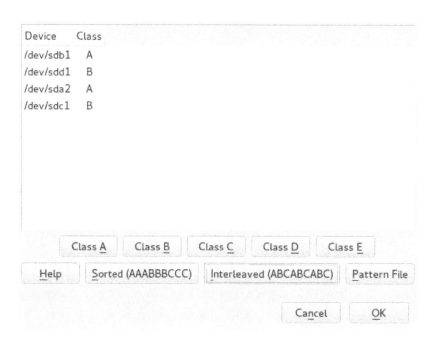

8. Click *Next*.

9. Under *RAID Options*, specify the *Chunk Size* and *Parity Algorithm*, then click *Next*.

For a RAID 10, the parity options are n (near), f (far), and o (offset). The number indicates the number of replicas of each data block that are required. Two is the default. For information, see *Section 8.2.2, "Layout"*.

10. Add a file system and mount options to the RAID device, then click *Finish*.

11. Click *Next*.

12. Verify the changes to be made, then click *Finish* to create the RAID.

8.2.4 Creating a Complex RAID 10 with mdadm

The procedure in this section uses the device names shown in the following table. Ensure that you modify the device names with the names of your own devices.

TABLE 8.5: SCENARIO FOR CREATING A RAID 10 USING MDADM

Raw Devices	RAID 10
/dev/sdf1	/dev/md3
/dev/sdg1	
/dev/sdh1	
/dev/sdi1	

1. Open a terminal console.

2. If necessary, create at least four 0xFD Linux RAID partitions of equal size using a disk partitioner such as parted.

3. Create a RAID 10 by entering the following command.

```
mdadm --create /dev/md3 --run --level=10 --chunk=32 --raid-devices=4 \
/dev/sdf1 /dev/sdg1 /dev/sdh1 /dev/sdi1
```

Make sure to adjust the value for `--raid-devices` and the list of partitions according to your setup.

The command creates an array with near layout and two replicas. To change any of the two values, use the `--layout` as described in *Section 8.2.2.4, "Specifying the number of Replicas and the Layout with YaST and mdadm"*.

4. Create a file system on the RAID 10 device /dev/md3, for example an XFS file system:

```
sudo mkfs.xfs /dev/md3
```

Modify the command if you want to use a different file system.

5. Edit the /etc/mdadm.conf file or create it, if it does not exist (for example by running **sudo vi /etc/mdadm.conf**). Add the following lines (if the file exists, the first line probably already exists, too) .

```
DEVICE containers partitions
ARRAY /dev/md3 UUID=UUID
```

The UUID of the device can be retrieved with the following command:

```
sudo mdadm -D /dev/md3 | grep UUID
```

6. Edit the /etc/fstab file to add an entry for the RAID 10 device /dev/md3. The following example shows an entry for a RAID device with the XFS file system and /data as a mount point.

```
/dev/md3 /data xfs defaults 1 2
```

7. Mount the RAID device:

```
sudo mount /data
```

9 Creating a Degraded RAID Array

A degraded array is one in which some devices are missing. Degraded arrays are supported only for RAID 1, RAID 4, RAID 5, and RAID 6. These RAID types are designed to withstand some missing devices as part of their fault-tolerance features. Typically, degraded arrays occur when a device fails. It is possible to create a degraded array on purpose.

RAID Type	Allowable Number of Slots Missing
RAID 1	All but one device
RAID 4	One slot
RAID 5	One slot
RAID 6	One or two slots

To create a degraded array in which some devices are missing, simply give the word `missing` in place of a device name. This causes **mdadm** to leave the corresponding slot in the array empty.

When creating a RAID 5 array, **mdadm** automatically creates a degraded array with an extra spare drive. This is because building the spare into a degraded array is generally faster than resynchronizing the parity on a non-degraded, but not clean, array. You can override this feature with the `--force` option.

Creating a degraded array might be useful if you want create a RAID, but one of the devices you want to use already has data on it. In that case, you create a degraded array with other devices, copy data from the in-use device to the RAID that is running in degraded mode, add the device into the RAID, then wait while the RAID is rebuilt so that the data is now across all devices. An example of this process is given in the following procedure:

1. To create a degraded RAID 1 device `/dev/md0`, using one single drive `/dev/sd1`, enter the following at the command prompt:

   ```
   mdadm --create /dev/md0 -l 1 -n 2 /dev/sda1 missing
   ```

   The device should be the same size or larger than the device you plan to add to it.

2. If the device you want to add to the mirror contains data that you want to move to the RAID array, copy it now to the RAID array while it is running in degraded mode.

3. Add the device you copied the data from to the mirror. For example, to add `/dev/sdb1` to the RAID, enter the following at the command prompt:

```
mdadm /dev/md0 -a /dev/sdb1
```

You can add only one device at a time. You must wait for the kernel to build the mirror and bring it fully online before you add another mirror.

4. Monitor the build progress by entering the following at the command prompt:

```
cat /proc/mdstat
```

To see the rebuild progress while being refreshed every second, enter

```
watch -n 1 cat /proc/mdstat
```

10 Resizing Software RAID Arrays with mdadm

This section describes how to increase or reduce the size of a software RAID 1, 4, 5, or 6 device with the Multiple Device Administration (`mdadm(8)`) tool.

Resizing an existing software RAID device involves increasing or decreasing the space contributed by each component partition. The file system that resides on the RAID must also be able to be resized to take advantage of the changes in available space on the device. In SUSE Linux Enterprise Server, file system resizing utilities are available for file systems Btrfs, Ext2, Ext3, Ext4, ReiserFS, and XFS (increase size only). Refer to *Chapter 2, Resizing File Systems* for more information.

The `mdadm` tool supports resizing only for software RAID levels 1, 4, 5, and 6. These RAID levels provide disk fault tolerance so that one component partition can be removed at a time for resizing. In principle, it is possible to perform a hot resize for RAID partitions, but you must take extra care for your data when doing so.

 Warning: Back Up your Data Before Resizing

Resizing any partition or file system involves some risks that can potentially result in losing data. To avoid data loss, ensure that you back up your data before you begin any resizing task.

Resizing the RAID involves the following tasks. The order in which these tasks are performed depends on whether you are increasing or decreasing its size.

TABLE 10.1: TASKS INVOLVED IN RESIZING A RAID

Tasks	Description	Order If Increasing Size	Order If Decreasing Size
Resize each of the component partitions.	Increase or decrease the active size of each component partition. You remove only one component partition at a time, modify its size, then return it to the RAID.	1	2

Tasks	Description	Order If Increasing Size	Order If Decreasing Size
Resize the software RAID itself.	The RAID does not automatically know about the increases or decreases you make to the underlying component partitions. You must inform it about the new size.	2	3
Resize the file system.	You must resize the file system that resides on the RAID. This is possible only for file systems that provide tools for resizing.	3	1

The procedures in the following sections use the device names shown in the following table. Ensure that you modify the names to use the names of your own devices.

TABLE 10.2: SCENARIO FOR INCREASING THE SIZE OF COMPONENT PARTITIONS

RAID Device	Component Partitions
/dev/md0	/dev/sda1
	/dev/sdb1
	/dev/sdc1

10.1   Increasing the Size of a Software RAID

Increasing the size of a software RAID involves the following tasks in the given order: increase the size of all partitions the RAID consists of, increase the size of the RAID itself and, finally, increase the size of the file system.

 Warning: Potential Data Loss

If a RAID does not have disk fault tolerance, or it is simply not consistent, data loss results if you remove any of its partitions. Be very careful when removing partitions, and ensure that you have a backup of your data available.

10.1.1 Increasing the Size of Component Partitions

Apply the procedure in this section to increase the size of a RAID 1, 4, 5, or 6. For each component partition in the RAID, remove the partition from the RAID, modify its size, return it to the RAID, then wait until the RAID stabilizes to continue. While a partition is removed, the RAID operates in degraded mode and has no or reduced disk fault tolerance. Even for RAIDs that can tolerate multiple concurrent disk failures, do not remove more than one component partition at a time. To increase the size of the component partitions for the RAID, proceed as follows:

1. Open a terminal console.

2. Ensure that the RAID array is consistent and synchronized by entering

   ```
   cat /proc/mdstat
   ```

   If your RAID array is still synchronizing according to the output of this command, you must wait until synchronization is complete before continuing.

3. Remove one of the component partitions from the RAID array. For example, to remove /dev/sda1, enter

   ```
   sudo mdadm /dev/md0 --fail /dev/sda1 --remove /dev/sda1
   ```

   To succeed, both the fail and remove actions must be specified.

4. Increase the size of the partition that you removed in the previous step by doing one of the following:

   - Increase the size of the partition, using a disk partitioner such as the YaST Partitioner or the command line tool parted. This option is the usual choice.

   - Replace the disk on which the partition resides with a higher-capacity device. This option is possible only if no other file systems on the original disk are accessed by the system. When the replacement device is added back into the RAID, it takes much longer to synchronize the data because all of the data that was on the original device must be rebuilt.

5. Re-add the partition to the RAID array. For example, to add /dev/sda1, enter

   ```
   sudo mdadm -a /dev/md0 /dev/sda1
   ```

Wait until the RAID is synchronized and consistent before continuing with the next partition.

6. Repeat these steps for each of the remaining component devices in the array. Ensure that you modify the commands for the correct component partition.

7. If you get a message that tells you that the kernel could not re-read the partition table for the RAID, you must reboot the computer after all partitions have been resized to force an update of the partition table.

8. Continue with *Section 10.1.2, "Increasing the Size of the RAID Array"*.

10.1.2   Increasing the Size of the RAID Array

After you have resized each of the component partitions in the RAID (see *Section 10.1.1, "Increasing the Size of Component Partitions"*), the RAID array configuration continues to use the original array size until you force it to be aware of the newly available space. You can specify a size for the RAID or use the maximum available space.

The procedure in this section uses the device name /dev/md0 for the RAID device. Ensure that you modify the name to use the name of your own device.

1. Open a terminal console.

2. Ensure that the RAID array is consistent and synchronized by entering

```
cat /proc/mdstat
```

If your RAID array is still synchronizing according to the output of this command, you must wait until synchronization is complete before continuing.

3. Check the size of the array and the device size known to the array by entering

```
sudo mdadm -D /dev/md0 | grep -e "Array Size" -e "Dev Size"
```

4. Do one of the following:

   • Increase the size of the array to the maximum available size by entering

```
sudo mdadm --grow /dev/md0 -z max
```

- Increase the size of the array to the maximum available size by entering

```
sudo mdadm --grow /dev/md0 -z max --assume-clean
```

The array uses any space that has been added to the devices, but this space will not be synchronized. This is recommended for RAID 1 because the synchronisation is not needed. It can be useful for other RAID levels if the space that was added to the member devices was pre-zeroed.

- Increase the size of the array to a specified value by entering

```
sudo mdadm --grow /dev/md0 -z size
```

Replace _size_ with an integer value in kilobytes (a kilobyte is 1024 bytes) for the desired size.

5. Recheck the size of your array and the device size known to the array by entering

```
sudo mdadm -D /dev/md0 | grep -e "Array Size" -e "Dev Size"
```

6. Do one of the following:

- If your array was successfully resized, continue with _Section 10.1.3, "Increasing the Size of the File System"_.

- If your array was not resized as you expected, you must reboot, then try this procedure again.

10.1.3   Increasing the Size of the File System

After you increase the size of the array (see _Section 10.1.2, "Increasing the Size of the RAID Array"_), you are ready to resize the file system.

You can increase the size of the file system to the maximum space available or specify an exact size. When specifying an exact size for the file system, ensure that the new size satisfies the following conditions:

- The new size must be greater than the size of the existing data; otherwise, data loss occurs.

- The new size must be equal to or less than the current RAID size because the file system size cannot extend beyond the space available.

Refer to *Chapter 2, Resizing File Systems* for detailed instructions.

10.2 Decreasing the Size of a Software RAID

Decreasing the Size of a Software RAID involves the following tasks in the given order: decrease the size of the file system, decrease the size of all partitions the RAID consists of, and finally decrease the size of the RAID itself.

Warning: Potential Data Loss

If a RAID does not have disk fault tolerance, or it is simply not consistent, data loss results if you remove any of its partitions. Be very careful when removing partitions, and ensure that you have a backup of your data available.

Important: XFS

Decreasing the size of a file system formatted with XFS is not possible, since such a feature is not supported by XFS. As a consequence, the size of a RAID that uses the XFS file system cannot be decreased.

10.2.1 Decreasing the Size of the File System

When decreasing the size of the file system on a RAID device, ensure that the new size satisfies the following conditions:

- The new size must be greater than the size of the existing data; otherwise, data loss occurs.

- The new size must be equal to or less than the current RAID size because the file system size cannot extend beyond the space available.

Refer to *Chapter 2, Resizing File Systems* for detailed instructions.

10.2.2 Decreasing the Size of the RAID Array

After you have resized the file system (see *Section 10.2.1, "Decreasing the Size of the File System"*), the RAID array configuration continues to use the original array size until you force it to reduce the available space. Use the **mdadm --grow** mode to force the RAID to use a smaller segment size. To do this, you must use the -z option to specify the amount of space in kilobytes to use from each device in the RAID. This size must be a multiple of the chunk size, and it must leave about 128 KB of space for the RAID superblock to be written to the device.

The procedure in this section uses the device name /dev/md0 for the RAID device. Ensure that you modify commands to use the name of your own device.

1. Open a terminal console.

2. Check the size of the array and the device size known to the array by entering

   ```
   sudo mdadm -D /dev/md0 | grep -e "Array Size" -e "Dev Size"
   ```

3. Decrease the array's device size to a specified value by entering

   ```
   sudo mdadm --grow /dev/md0 -z size
   ```

   Replace *size* with an integer value in kilobytes for the desired size. (A kilobyte is 1024 bytes.)
   For example, the following command sets the segment size for each RAID device to about 40 GB where the chunk size is 64 KB. It includes 128 KB for the RAID superblock.

   ```
   sudo mdadm --grow /dev/md2 -z 41943168
   ```

4. Recheck the size of your array and the device size known to the array by entering

   ```
   sudo mdadm -D /dev/md0 | grep -e "Array Size" -e "Device Size"
   ```

5. Do one of the following:

- If your array was successfully resized, continue with *Section 10.2.3, "Decreasing the Size of Component Partitions"*.

- If your array was not resized as you expected, you must reboot, then try this procedure again.

10.2.3   Decreasing the Size of Component Partitions

After you decrease the segment size that is used on each device in the RAID (see *Section 10.2.2, "Decreasing the Size of the RAID Array"*), the remaining space in each component partition is not used by the RAID. You can leave partitions at their current size to allow for the RAID to grow at a future time, or you can reclaim this now unused space.

To reclaim the space, you decrease the component partitions one at a time. For each component partition, you remove it from the RAID, reduce its partition size, return the partition to the RAID, then wait until the RAID stabilizes. To allow for metadata, you should specify a slightly larger size than the size you specified for the RAID in *Section 10.2.2, "Decreasing the Size of the RAID Array"*.

While a partition is removed, the RAID operates in degraded mode and has no or reduced disk fault tolerance. Even for RAIDs that can tolerate multiple concurrent disk failures, you should never remove more than one component partition at a time. To decrease the size of the component partitions for the RAID, proceed as follows:

1. Open a terminal console.

2. Ensure that the RAID array is consistent and synchronized by entering

   ```
   cat /proc/mdstat
   ```

   If your RAID array is still synchronizing according to the output of this command, you must wait until synchronization is complete before continuing.

3. Remove one of the component partitions from the RAID array. For example, to remove /dev/sda1, enter

   ```
   sudo mdadm /dev/md0 --fail /dev/sda1 --remove /dev/sda1
   ```

   To succeed, both the fail and remove actions must be specified.

4. Decrease the size of the partition that you removed in the previous step to a size that is slightly larger than the size you set for the segment size. The size should be a multiple of the chunk size and allow 128 KB for the RAID superblock. Use a disk partitioner such as the YaST partitioner or the command line tool parted to decrease the size of the partition.

5. Re-add the partition to the RAID array. For example, to add /dev/sda1, enter

```
sudo mdadm -a /dev/md0 /dev/sda1
```

Wait until the RAID is synchronized and consistent before continuing with the next partition.

6. Repeat these steps for each of the remaining component devices in the array. Ensure that you modify the commands for the correct component partition.

7. If you get a message that tells you that the kernel could not re-read the partition table for the RAID, you must reboot the computer after resizing all of its component partitions.

8. (Optional) Expand the size of the RAID and file system to use the maximum amount of space in the now smaller component partitions and increase the size of the file system afterwards. Refer to *Section 10.1.2, "Increasing the Size of the RAID Array"* for instructions.

11 Storage Enclosure LED Utilities for MD Software RAIDs

Storage enclosure LED Monitoring utility (`ledmon`) and LED Control (`ledctl`) utility are Linux user space applications that use a broad range of interfaces and protocols to control storage enclosure LEDs. The primary usage is to visualize the status of Linux MD software RAID devices created with the mdadm utility. The `ledmon` daemon monitors the status of the drive array and updates the status of the drive LEDs. The ledctl utility allows you to set LED patterns for specified devices.

These LED utilities use the SGPIO (Serial General Purpose Input/Output) specification (Small Form Factor (SFF) 8485) and the SCSI Enclosure Services (SES) 2 protocol to control LEDs. They implement the International Blinking Pattern Interpretation (IBPI) patterns of the SFF-8489 specification for SGPIO. The IBPI defines how the SGPIO standards are interpreted as states for drives and slots on a backplane and how the backplane should visualize the states with LEDs.

Some storage enclosures do not adhere strictly to the SFF-8489 specification. An enclosure processor might accept an IBPI pattern but not blink the LEDs according to the SFF-8489 specification, or the processor might support only a limited number of the IBPI patterns.

LED management (AHCI) and SAF-TE protocols are not supported by the `ledmon` and `ledctl` utilities.

The `ledmon` and `ledctl` applications have been verified to work with Intel storage controllers such as the Intel AHCI controller and Intel SAS controller. They also support PCIe-SSD (solid state drive) enclosure LEDs to control the storage enclosure status (OK, Fail, Rebuilding) LEDs of PCIe-SSD devices that are part of an MD software RAID volume. The applications might also work with the IBPI-compliant storage controllers of other vendors (especially SAS/SCSI controllers); however, other vendors' controllers have not been tested.

`ledmon` and `ledctl` are part of the `ledmon` package, which is not installed by default. Run **`sudo zypper in ledmon`** to install it.

11.1 The Storage Enclosure LED Monitor Service

The `ledmon` application is a daemon process that constantly monitors the state of MD software RAID devices or the state of block devices in a storage enclosure or drive bay. Only a single instance of the daemon should be running at a time. The `ledmon` daemon is part of Intel Enclosure LED Utilities.

The state is visualized on LEDs associated with each slot in a storage array enclosure or a drive bay. The application monitors all software RAID devices and visualizes their state. It does not provide a way to monitor only selected software RAID volumes.

The `ledmon` daemon supports two types of LED systems: A two-LED system (Activity LED and Status LED) and a three-LED system (Activity LED, Locate LED, and Fail LED). This tool has the highest priority when accessing the LEDs.

To start `ledmon`, enter

```
sudo ledmon [options]
```

where [options] is one or more of the following:

OPTIONS FOR `ledmon`

-c,
--confg=path

> The configuration is read from `~/.ledctl` or from `/etc/ledcfg.conf` if existing. Use this option to specify an alternative configuration file.
>
> Currently this option has no effect, since support for configuration files has not been implemented yet. See **man 5 ledctl.conf** for details.

-l,
--log=path

> Sets a path to local log file. If this user-defined file is specified, the global log file `/var/log/ledmon.log` is not used.

-t,
--interval=seconds

> Sets the time interval between scans of `sysfs`. The value is given in seconds. The minimum is 5 seconds. The maximum is not specified.

[--quiet|--error|--warning|--info|--debug|--all]

Specifies the verbosity level. The level options are specified in the order of no information to the most information. Use the --quiet option for no logging. Use the --all option to log everything. If you specify more than one verbose option, the last option in the command applies.

-h,
--help

Prints the command information to the console, then exits.

-v,
--version

Displays version of **ledmon** and information about the license, then exits.

 Note: Known Issues

The **ledmon** daemon does not recognize the PFA (Predicted Failure Analysis) state from the SFF-8489 specification. Thus, the PFA pattern is not visualized.

11.2   The Storage Enclosure LED Control Application

The Enclosure LED Application (**ledctl**) is a user space application that controls LEDs associated with each slot in a storage enclosure or a drive bay. The **ledctl** application is a part of Intel Enclosure LED Utilities.

When you issue the command, the LEDs of the specified devices are set to a specified pattern and all other LEDs are turned off. This application needs to be run with root privileges. Because the ledmon application has the highest priority when accessing LEDs, some patterns set by ledctl might have no effect if the ledmon daemon is running (except for the Locate pattern).

The **ledctl** application supports two types of LED systems: A two-LED system (Activity LED and Status LED) and a three-LED system (Activity LED, Fail LED, and Locate LED).

To start **ledctl**, enter

```
sudo [options] pattern_name=list_of_devices
```

where [options] is one or more of the following:

-c,

--confg=path

    Sets a path to local configuration file. If this option is specified, the global configuration file and user configuration file have no effect.

-l,

--log=path

    Sets a path to local log file. If this user-defined file is specified, the global log file `/var/log/ledmon.log` is not used.

--quiet

    Turns off all messages sent to `stdout` or `stderr` out. The messages are still logged to local file and the `syslog` facility.

-h,

--help

    Prints the command information to the console, then exits.

-v,

--version

    Displays version of **ledctl** and information about the license, then exits.

11.2.1 Pattern Names

The **ledctl** application accepts the following names for *pattern_name* argument, according to the SFF-8489 specification.

locate

    Turns on the Locate LED associated with the specified devices or empty slots. This state is used to identify a slot or drive.

locate_off

    Turns off the Locate LED associated with the specified devices or empty slots.

normal

    Turns off the Status LED, Failure LED, and Locate LED associated with the specified devices.

off

> Turns off only the Status LED and Failure LED associated with the specified devices.

ica,

degraded

> Visualizes the `In a Critical Array` pattern.

rebuild,

rebuild_p

> Visualizes the `Rebuild` pattern. This supports both of the rebuild states for compatibility and legacy reasons.

ifa,

failed_array

> Visualizes the `In a Failed Array` pattern.

hotspare

> Visualizes the `Hotspare` pattern.

pfa

> Visualizes the `Predicted Failure Analysis` pattern.

failure,

disk_failed

> Visualizes the `Failure` pattern.

ses_abort

> SES-2 R/R ABORT

ses_rebuild

> SES-2 REBUILD/REMAP

ses_ifa

> SES-2 IN FAILED ARRAY

ses_ica

> SES-2 IN CRITICAL ARRAY

ses_cons_check

> SES-2 CONS CHECK

ses_hotspare

> SES-2 HOTSPARE

ses_rsvd_dev

    SES-2 RSVD DEVICE

ses_ok

    SES-2 OK

ses_ident

    SES-2 IDENT

ses_rm

    SES-2 REMOVE

ses_insert

    SES-2 INSERT

ses_missing

    SES-2 MISSING

ses_dnr

    SES-2 DO NOT REMOVE

ses_active

    SES-2 ACTIVE

ses_enable_bb

    SES-2 ENABLE BYP B

ses_enable_ba

    SES-2 ENABLE BYP A

ses_devoff

    SES-2 DEVICE OFF

ses_fault

    SES-2 FAULT

When a non-SES-2 pattern is sent to a device in an enclosure, the pattern is automatically translated to the SCSI Enclosure Services (SES) 2 pattern as shown above.

TABLE 11.1: TRANSLATION BETWEEN NON-SES-2 PATTERNS AND SES-2 PATTERNS

Non-SES-2 Pattern	SES-2 Pattern
locate	ses_ident

Pattern Names

Non-SES-2 Pattern	SES-2 Pattern
locate_off	ses_ident
normal	ses_ok
off	ses_ok
ica	ses_ica
degraded	ses_ica
rebuild	ses_rebuild
rebuild_p	ses_rebuild
ifa	ses_ifa
failed_array	ses_ifa
hotspare	ses_hotspare
pfa	ses_rsvd_dev
failure	ses_fault
disk_failed	ses_fault

11.2.2   List of Devices

When you issue the **ledctl** command, the LEDs of the specified devices are set to the specified pattern and all other LEDs are turned off. The list of devices can be provided in one of two formats:

- A list of devices separated by a comma and no spaces

- A list in curly braces with devices separated by a space

If you specify multiple patterns in the same command, the device list for each pattern can use the same or different format. For examples that show the two list formats, see *Section 11.2.3, "Examples"*.

A device is a path to file in the /dev directory or in the /sys/block directory. The path can identify a block device, an MD software RAID device, or a container device. For a software RAID device or a container device, the reported LED state is set for all of the associated block devices.

The LEDs of devices listed in list_of_devices are set to the given pattern pattern_name and all other LEDs are turned off.

11.2.3 Examples

To locate a single block device:

```
sudo ledctl locate=/dev/sda
```

To turn off the Locate LED for a single block device:

```
sudo ledctl locate_off=/dev/sda
```

To locate disks of an MD software RAID device and to set a rebuild pattern for two of its block devices at the same time:

```
sudo ledctl locate=/dev/md127 rebuild={ /sys/block/sd[a-b] }
```

To turn off the Status LED and Failure LED for the specified devices:

```
sudo ledctl off={ /dev/sda /dev/sdb }
```

To locate three block devices run one of the following commends (both are equivalent):

```
sudo ledctl locate=/dev/sda,/dev/sdb,/dev/sdc
sudo ledctl locate={ /dev/sda /dev/sdb /dev/sdc }
```

11.3 Additional Information

See the following resources for details about the LED patterns and monitoring tools:

- LEDMON open source project on Sourceforge.net [http://sourceforge.net/projects/led-mon/]

- SGPIO specification SFF-8485 [ftp://ftp.seagate.com/sff/SFF-8485.PDF]

- IBPI specification SFF-8489 [ftp://ftp.seagate.com/sff/SFF-8489.PDF]

IV Network Storage

12 iSNS for Linux

Storage area networks (SANs) can contain many disk drives that are dispersed across complex networks. This can make device discovery and device ownership difficult. iSCSI initiators must be able to identify storage resources in the SAN and determine whether they have access to them.

Internet Storage Name Service (iSNS) is a standards-based service that simplifies the automated discovery, management, and configuration of iSCSI devices on a TCP/IP network. iSNS provides intelligent storage discovery and management services comparable to those found in Fibre Channel networks.

 Important: Security Considerations

iSNS should be used only in secure internal networks.

12.1 How iSNS Works

For an iSCSI initiator to discover iSCSI targets, it needs to identify which devices in the network are storage resources and what IP addresses it needs to access them. A query to an iSNS server returns a list of iSCSI targets and the IP addresses that the initiator has permission to access.

Using iSNS, you create iSNS discovery domains into which you then group or organize iSCSI targets and initiators. By dividing storage nodes into domains, you can limit the discovery process of each host to the most appropriate subset of targets registered with iSNS, which allows the storage network to scale by reducing the number of unnecessary discoveries and by limiting the amount of time each host spends establishing discovery relationships. This lets you control and simplify the number of targets and initiators that must be discovered.

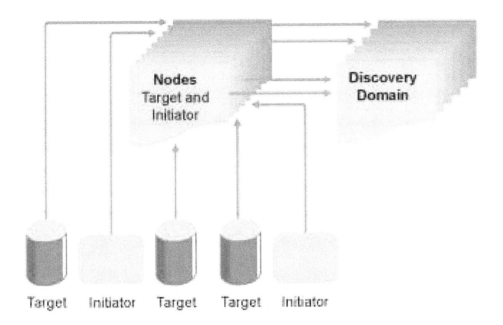

FIGURE 12.1: ISNS DISCOVERY DOMAINS

Both iSCSI targets and iSCSI initiators use iSNS clients to initiate transactions with iSNS servers by using the iSNS protocol. They then register device attribute information in a common discovery domain, download information about other registered clients, and receive asynchronous notification of events that occur in their discovery domain.

iSNS servers respond to iSNS protocol queries and requests made by iSNS clients using the iSNS protocol. iSNS servers initiate iSNS protocol state change notifications and store properly authenticated information submitted by a registration request in an iSNS database.

Benefits provided by iSNS for Linux include:

- Provides an information facility for registration, discovery, and management of networked storage assets.

- Integrates with the DNS infrastructure.

- Consolidates registration, discovery, and management of iSCSI storage.

- Simplifies storage management implementations.

- Improves scalability compared to other discovery methods.

An example of the benefits iSNS provides can be better understood through the following scenario:

Suppose you have a company that has 100 iSCSI initiators and 100 iSCSI targets. Depending on your configuration, all iSCSI initiators could potentially try to discover and connect to any of the 100 iSCSI targets. This could create discovery and connection difficulties. By grouping initiators and targets into discovery domains, you can prevent iSCSI initiators in one department from discovering the iSCSI targets in another department. The result is that the iSCSI initiators in a specific department only discover those iSCSI targets that are part of the department's discovery domain.

12.2   Installing iSNS Server for Linux

iSNS Server for Linux is included with SUSE Linux Enterprise Server, but is not installed or configured by default. You need to install the package `open-isns` and configure the iSNS service.

 Note: iSNS and iSCSI on the Same Server

iSNS can be installed on the same server where iSCSI target or iSCSI initiator software is installed. Installing both the iSCSI target software and iSCSI initiator software on the same server is not supported.

To install iSNS for Linux:

1. Start YaST and select *Network Services* › *iSNS Server*.

2. In case `open-isns` is not installed yet, you are prompted to install it now. Confirm by clicking *Install*.

3. The iSNS Service configuration dialog opens automatically to the *Service* tab.

4. In *Service Start*, select one of the following:

 - **When Booting:** The iSNS service starts automatically on server start-up.

 - **Manually (Default):** The iSNS service must be started manually by entering `sudo systemctl start isnsd` at the server console of the server where you install it.

5. Specify the following firewall settings:

 - **Open Port in Firewall:** Select the check box to open the firewall and allow access to the service from remote computers. The firewall port is closed by default.

 - **Firewall Details:** If you open the firewall port, the port is open on all network interfaces by default. Click *Firewall Details* to select interfaces on which to open the port, select the network interfaces to use, then click *OK*.

6. Click *OK* to apply the configuration settings and complete the installation.

7. Continue with *Section 12.3, "Configuring iSNS Discovery Domains"*.

12.3   Configuring iSNS Discovery Domains

In order for iSCSI initiators and targets to use the iSNS service, they must belong to a discovery domain.

 Important: The iSNS Service Must be Active

The iSNS service must be installed and running to configure iSNS discovery domains. For information, see *Section 12.4, "Starting the iSNS Service"*.

12.3.1   Creating iSNS Discovery Domains

A default discovery domain named *default DD* is automatically created when you install the iSNS service. The existing iSCSI targets and initiators that have been configured to use iSNS are automatically added to the default discovery domain.

To create a new discovery domain:

1. Start YaST and under *Network Services*, select *iSNS Server*.

2. Click the *Discovery Domains* tab.

   The *Discovery Domains* area lists all existing discovery domains. You can *Create Discovery Domains*, or *Delete* existing ones. Deleting a domain removes the members from the domain, but it does not delete the iSCSI node members.

   The *Discovery Domain Members* area lists all iSCSI nodes assigned to a selected discovery domain. Selecting a different discovery domain refreshes the list with members from that discovery domain. You can add and delete iSCSI nodes from a selected discovery domain. Deleting an iSCSI node removes it from the domain, but it does not delete the iSCSI node. *Create iSCSI Node Member* allows a node that is not yet registered to be added as a member of the discovery domain. When the iSCSI initiator or target registers this node, then it becomes part of this domain.

   When an iSCSI initiator performs a discovery request, the iSNS service returns all iSCSI node targets that are members of the same discovery domain.

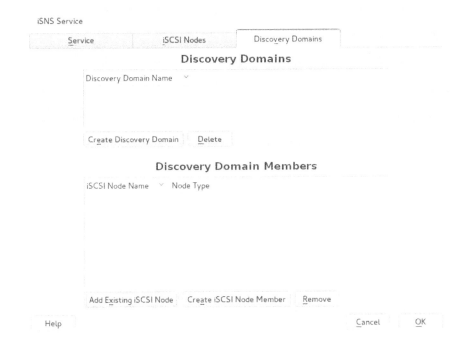

3. Click the *Create Discovery Domain* button.

   You can also select an existing discovery domain and click the *Delete* button to remove that discovery domain.

4. Specify the name of the discovery domain you are creating, then click *OK*.

5. Continue with *Section 12.3.2, "Adding iSCSI Nodes to a Discovery Domain".*

12.3.2   Adding iSCSI Nodes to a Discovery Domain

1. Start YaST and under *Network Services*, select *iSNS Server*.

2. Click the *iSCSI Nodes* tab.

3. Review the list of nodes to ensure that the iSCSI targets and initiators that you want to use the iSNS service are listed.

If an iSCSI target or initiator is not listed, you might need to restart the iSCSI service on the node. You can do this by running

```
sudo systemctl restart iscsid.socket
sudo systemctl restart iscsi
```

to restart an initiator or

```
sudo systemctl restart target-isns
```

to restart a target.

You can select an iSCSI node and click the *Delete* button to remove that node from the iSNS database. This is useful if you are no longer using an iSCSI node or have renamed it. The iSCSI node is automatically added to the list (iSNS database) again when you restart the iSCSI service or reboot the server unless you remove or comment out the iSNS portion of the iSCSI configuration file.

4. Click the *Discovery Domains* tab and select the desired discovery domain.

5. Click *Add existing iSCSI Node*, select the node you want to add to the domain, then click *Add Node*.

6. Repeat the previous step for as many nodes as you want to add to the discovery domain, then click *Done* when you are finished adding nodes.

Note that an iSCSI node can belong to more than one discovery domain.

12.4 Starting the iSNS Service

iSNS must be started at the server where you install it. If you have not configured it to be started at boot time (see *Section 12.2, "Installing iSNS Server for Linux"* for details), enter the following command at a terminal console:

```
sudo systemctl start isnsd
```

You can also use the **stop**, **status**, and **restart** options with iSNS.

12.5 For More Information

For information, see the *Linux iSNS for iSCSI project* at http://sourceforge.net/projects/linuxisns/. The electronic mailing list for this project can be found at http://sourceforge.net/mailarchive/forum.php?forum_name=linuxisns-discussion.

General information about iSNS is available in *RFC 4171: Internet Storage Name Service* at http://www.ietf.org/rfc/rfc4171.

13 Mass Storage over IP Networks: iSCSI

One of the central tasks in computer centers and when operating servers is providing hard disk capacity for server systems. Fibre Channel is often used for this purpose. iSCSI (Internet SCSI) solutions provide a lower-cost alternative to Fibre Channel that can leverage commodity servers and Ethernet networking equipment. Linux iSCSI provides iSCSI initiator and iSCSI LIO target software for connecting Linux servers to central storage systems.

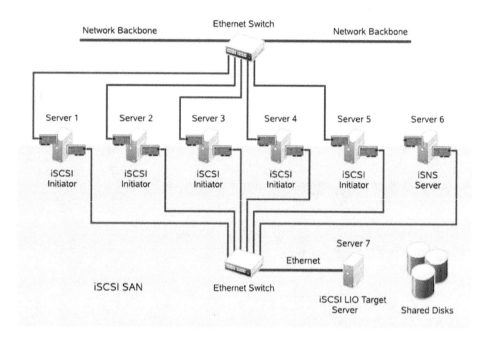

FIGURE 13.1: ISCSI SAN WITH AN ISNS SERVER

 Note: LIO

LIO (http://linux-iscsi.org) is the standard open source multiprotocol SCSI target for Linux. LIO replaced the STGT (SCSI Target) framework as the standard unified storage target in Linux with Linux kernel version 2.6.38 and later. In SUSE Linux Enterprise Server 12 the iSCSI LIO Target Server replaces the iSCSI Target Server from previous versions.

iSCSI is a storage networking protocol that facilitates data transfers of SCSI packets over TCP/IP networks between block storage devices and servers. iSCSI target software runs on the target server and defines the logical units as iSCSI target devices. iSCSI initiator software runs on different servers and connects to the target devices to make the storage devices available on that server.

The iSCSI LIO target server and iSCSI initiator servers communicate by sending SCSI packets at the IP level in your LAN. When an application running on the initiator server starts an inquiry for an iSCSI LIO target device, the operating system produces the necessary SCSI commands. The SCSI commands are then embedded in IP packets and encrypted as necessary by software that is commonly known as the *iSCSI initiator*. The packets are transferred across the internal IP network to the corresponding iSCSI remote station, called the *iSCSI LIO target server*, or simply the *iSCSI target*.

Many storage solutions provide access over iSCSI, but it is also possible to run a Linux server that provides an iSCSI target. In this case, it is important to set up a Linux server that is optimized for file system services. The iSCSI target accesses block devices in Linux. Therefore, it is possible to use RAID solutions to increase disk space and a lot of memory to improve data caching. For more information about RAID, also see *Chapter 6, Software RAID Configuration*.

13.1   Installing the iSCSI LIO Target Server and iSCSI Initiator

While the iSCSI initiator is installed by default (packages `open-iscsi` and `yast2-iscsi-client`), the iSCSI LIO target packages need to be installed manually.

 Important: Initiator and Target may not Run on the Same Server

It is not supported to run iSCSI target software and iSCSI initiator software on the same server in a production environment.

To install the iSCSI LIO Target Server, run the following command in a terminal console:

```
sudo zypper in yast2-iscsi-lio-server
```

In case you need to install the iSCSI initiator or any of its dependencies, run the command **sudo zypper in yast2-iscsi-client**.

Alternatively, use the YaST Software Management module for installation.

Any packages required in addition to the ones mentioned above will either be automatically pulled in by the installer, or be installed when you first run the respective YaST module.

13.2 Setting Up an iSCSI LIO Target Server

This section describes how to use YaST to configure an iSCSI LIO Target Server and set up iSCSI LIO target devices. You can use any iSCSI initiator software to access the target devices.

13.2.1 iSCSI LIO Target Service Start-up and Firewall Settings

The iSCSI LIO Target service is by default configured to be started manually. You can configure the service to start automatically at boot time. If you use a firewall on the server and you want the iSCSI LIO targets to be available to other computers, you must open a port in the firewall for each adapter that you want to use for target access. TCP port 3260 is the port number for the iSCSI protocol, as defined by IANA (Internet Assigned Numbers Authority).

1. Start YaST and launch *Network Services* › *iSCSI LIO Target*.

2. Switch to the *Service* tab.

3. Under *Service Start*, specify how you want the iSCSI LIO target service to be started:

- **When Booting:** The service starts automatically on server restart.

- **Manually:** (Default) You must start the service manually after a server restart by running `sudo systemctl start target`. The target devices are not available until you start the service.

4. If you use a firewall on the server and you want the iSCSI LIO targets to be available to other computers, open port 3260 in the firewall for each adapter interface that you want to use for target access. If the port is closed for all of the network interfaces, the iSCSI LIO targets are not available to other computers.

   If you do not use a firewall on the server, the firewall settings are disabled. In this case skip the following steps and leave the configuration dialog with *Finish* or switch to another tab to continue with the configuration.

   a. On the *Services* tab, select the *Open Port in Firewall* check box to enable the firewall settings.

   b. Click *Firewall Details* to view or configure the network interfaces to use. All available network interfaces are listed, and all are selected by default. Deselect all interfaces on which the port should *not* be opened. Save your settings with *OK*.

5. Click *Finish* to save and apply the iSCSI LIO Target service settings.

13.2.2 Configuring Authentication for Discovery of iSCSI LIO Targets and Clients

The iSCSI LIO Target Server software supports the PPP-CHAP (Point-to-Point Protocol Challenge Handshake Authentication Protocol), a three-way authentication method defined in the *Internet Engineering Task Force (IETF) RFC 1994* (http://www.ietf.org/rfc/rfc1994.txt). The server uses this authentication method for the discovery of iSCSI LIO targets and clients, not for accessing files on the targets. If you do not want to restrict the access to the discovery, use *No Authentication*. The *No Authentication* option is enabled by default. Without requiring authentication all iSCSI LIO targets on this server can be discovered by any iSCSI initiator client on the same network. This server can discover any iSCSI initiator client on the same network that does not require authentication for discovery.

If authentication is needed for a more secure configuration, you can use incoming authentication, outgoing authentication, or both. *Incoming Authentication* requires an iSCSI initiator to prove that it has the permissions to run a discovery on the iSCSI LIO target. The initiator must provide the incoming user name and password. *Outgoing Authentication* requires the iSCSI LIO target to prove to the initiator that it is the expected target. The iSCSI LIO target must provide the outgoing user name and password to the iSCSI initiator. The user name and password pair can be different for incoming and outgoing discovery. If authentication for discovery is enabled, its settings apply to all iSCSI LIO target groups.

 Important: Security

We recommend that you use authentication for target and client discovery in production environments for security reasons.

To configure authentication preferences for iSCSI LIO targets:

1. Start YaST and launch *Network Services* > *iSCSI LIO Target.*

2. Switch to the *Global* tab.

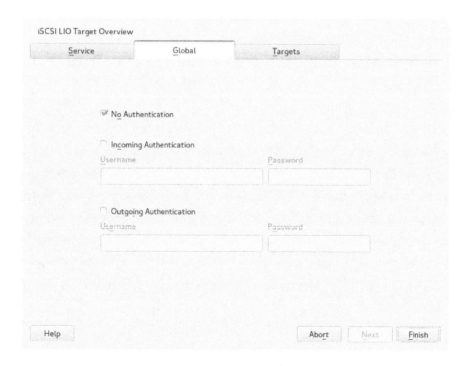

3. By default, authentication is disabled (*No Authentication*). To enable Authentication, select *Incoming Authentication, Outgoing Authentication* or both.

4. Provide credentials for the selected authentication method(s). The user name and password pair can be different for incoming and outgoing discovery.

5. Click *Finish* to save and apply the settings.

13.2.3   Preparing the Storage Space

The iSCSI LIO target configuration exports existing block devices to iSCSI initiators. You must prepare the storage space you want to use in the target devices by setting up unformatted partitions or devices by using the Partitioner in YaST, or by partitioning the devices from the command line with parted. iSCSI LIO targets can use unformatted partitions with Linux, Linux LVM, or Linux RAID file system IDs. Refer to *Book "Deployment Guide", Chapter 14 "Advanced Disk Setup", Section 14.1 "Using the YaST Partitioner"* for details.

Important: Do Not Mount iSCSI Target Devices

After you set up a device or partition for use as an iSCSI target, you never access it directly via its local path. Do not specify a mount point for it when you create it.

13.2.3.1   Partitioning Devices in a Virtual Environment

You can use a virtual machine guest server as an iSCSI LIO Target Server. This section describes how to assign partitions to a Xen virtual machine. You can also use other virtual environments that are supported by SUSE Linux Enterprise Server.

In a Xen virtual environment, you must assign the storage space you want to use for the iSCSI LIO target devices to the guest virtual machine, then access the space as virtual disks within the guest environment. Each virtual disk can be a physical block device, such as an entire disk, partition, or volume, or it can be a file-backed disk image where the virtual disk is a single image file on a larger physical disk on the Xen host server. For the best performance, create each virtual disk from a physical disk or a partition. After you set up the virtual disks for the guest virtual machine, start the guest server, then configure the new blank virtual disks as iSCSI target devices by following the same process as for a physical server.

File-backed disk images are created on the Xen host server, then assigned to the Xen guest server. By default, Xen stores file-backed disk images in the `/var/lib/xen/images/vm_name` directory, where *vm_name* is the name of the virtual machine.

13.2.4 Setting Up an iSCSI LIO Target Group

You can use YaST to configure iSCSI LIO target devices. YaST uses APIs provided by the **lio-utils** software. iSCSI LIO targets can use unformatted partitions with Linux, Linux LVM, or Linux RAID file system IDs.

 Important: Partitions

> Before you begin, create the unformatted partitions that you want to use as iSCSI LIO targets as described in *Section 13.2.3, "Preparing the Storage Space"*.

1. Start YaST and launch *Network Services* › *iSCSI LIO Target*.

2. Switch to the *Targets* tab.

3. Click *Add*, then define a new iSCSI LIO target group and devices:

The iSCSI LIO Target software automatically completes the *Target, Identifier, Portal Group, IP Address,* and *Port Number* fields. *Use Authentication* is selected by default.

a. If you have multiple network interfaces, use the IP address drop-down box to select the IP address of the network interface to use for this target group. To make the server accessible under all addresses, choose *Bind All IP Addresses*.

b. Deselect *Use Authentication* if you do not want to require client authentication for this target group (not recommended).

c. Click *Add*. Enter the path of the device or partition or *Browse* to add it. Optionally specify a name, then click *OK*. The LUN number is automatically generated, beginning with 0. A name is automatically generated if you leave the field empty.

d. (Optional) Repeat the previous steps to add more targets to this target group.

e. After all desired targets have been added to the group, click *Next*.

4. On the *Modify iSCSI Target Client Setup* page, configure information for the clients that are permitted to access LUNs in the target group:

After you specify at least one client for the target group, the *Edit LUN, Edit Auth, Delete,* and *Copy* buttons are enabled. You can use *Add* or *Copy* to add more clients for the target group:

MODIFY ISCSI TARGET: OPTIONS

- **Add:** Add a new client entry for the selected iSCSI LIO target group.

- **Edit LUN:** Configure which LUNs in the iSCSI LIO target group to map to a selected client. You can map each of the allocated targets to a preferred client LUN.

- **Edit Auth:** Configure the preferred authentication method for a selected client. You can specify no authentication, or you can configure incoming authentication, outgoing authentication, or both.

- **Delete:** Remove a selected client entry from the list of clients allocated to the target group.

- **Copy:** Add a new client entry with the same LUN mappings and authentication settings as a selected client entry. This allows you to easily allocate the same shared LUNs, in turn, to each node in a cluster.

a. Click *Add,* specify the client name, select or deselect the *Import LUNs from TPG* check box, then click *OK* to save the settings.

b. Select a client entry, click *Edit LUN,* modify the LUN mappings to specify which LUNs in the iSCSI LIO target group to allocate to the selected client, then click *OK* to save the changes.

   If the iSCSI LIO target group consists of multiple LUNs, you can allocate one or multiple LUNs to the selected client. By default, each of the available LUNs in the group are assigned to a client LUN.

   To modify the LUN allocation, perform one or more of the following actions:

   - **Add:** Click *Add* to create a new *Client LUN* entry, then use the *Change* drop-down box to map a target LUN to it.

   - **Delete:** Select the *Client LUN* entry, then click *Delete* to remove a target LUN mapping.

   - **Change:** Select the *Client LUN* entry, then use the *Change* drop-down box to select which Target LUN to map to it.

Setting Up an iSCSI LIO Target Group

Typical allocation plans include the following:

- A single server is listed as a client. All of the LUNs in the target group are allocated to it.

  You can use this grouping strategy to logically group the iSCSI SAN storage for a given server.

- Multiple independent servers are listed as clients. One or multiple target LUNs are allocated to each server. Each LUN is allocated to only one server.

  You can use this grouping strategy to logically group the iSCSI SAN storage for a given department or service category in the data center.

- Each node of a cluster is listed as a client. All of the shared target LUNs are allocated to each node. All nodes are attached to the devices, but for most file systems, the cluster software locks a device for access and mounts it on only one node at a time. Shared file systems (such as OCFS2) make it possible for multiple nodes to concurrently mount the same file structure and to open the same files with read and write access.

  You can use this grouping strategy to logically group the iSCSI SAN storage for a given server cluster.

c. Select a client entry, click *Edit Auth*, specify the authentication settings for the client, then click *OK* to save the settings.

   You can require *No Authentication*, or you can configure *Incoming Authentication*, *Outgoing Authentication*, or both. You can specify only one user name and password pair for each client. The credentials can be different for incoming and outgoing authentication for a client. The credentials can be different for each client.

d. Repeat the previous steps for each iSCSI client that can access this target group.

e. After the client assignments are configured, click *Next*.

5. Click *Finish* to save and apply the settings.

13.2.5   Modifying an iSCSI LIO Target Group

You can modify an existing iSCSI LIO target group as follows:

- Add or remove target LUN devices from a target group

- Add or remove clients for a target group

- Modify the client LUN-to-target LUN mappings for a client of a target group

- Modify the user name and password credentials for a client authentication (incoming, outgoing, or both)

To view or modify the settings for an iSCSI LIO target group:

1. Start YaST and launch *Network Services > iSCSI LIO Target*.

2. Switch to the *Targets* tab.

3. Select the iSCSI LIO target group to be modified, then click *Edit*.

4. On the Modify iSCSI Target LUN Setup page, add LUNs to the target group, edit the LUN assignments, or remove target LUNs from the group. After all desired changes have been made to the group, click *Next*.
   For option information, see *Modify iSCSI Target: Options*.

5. On the Modify iSCSI Target Client Setup page, configure information for the clients that are permitted to access LUNs in the target group. After all desired changes have been made to the group, click *Next*.

6. Click *Finish* to save and apply the settings.

13.2.6   Deleting an iSCSI LIO Target Group

Deleting an iSCSI LIO target group removes the definition of the group, and the related setup for clients, including LUN mappings and authentication credentials. It does not destroy the data on the partitions. To give clients access again, you can allocate the target LUNs to a different or new target group, and configure the client access for them.

1. Start YaST and launch *Network Services > iSCSI LIO Target*.

2. Switch to the *Targets* tab.

3. Select the iSCSI LIO target group to be deleted, then click *Delete*.

4. When you are prompted, click *Continue* to confirm the deletion, or click *Cancel* to cancel it.

5. Click *Finish* to save and apply the settings.

13.3 Configuring iSCSI Initiator

The iSCSI initiator, also called an iSCSI client, can be used to connect to any iSCSI target. This is not restricted to the iSCSI target solution explained in *Section 13.2, "Setting Up an iSCSI LIO Target Server"*. The configuration of iSCSI initiator involves two major steps: the discovery of available iSCSI targets and the setup of an iSCSI session. Both can be done with YaST.

13.3.1 Using YaST for the iSCSI Initiator Configuration

The iSCSI Initiator Overview in YaST is divided into three tabs:

Service:

The *Service* tab can be used to enable the iSCSI initiator at boot time. It also offers to set a unique *Initiator Name* and an iSNS server to use for the discovery. The default port for iSNS is 3205.

Connected Targets:

The *Connected Targets* tab gives an overview of the currently connected iSCSI targets. Like the *Discovered Targets* tab, it also gives the option to add new targets to the system.

On this page, you can select a target device, then toggle the start-up setting for each iSCSI target device:

Automatic: This option is used for iSCSI targets that are to be connected when the iSCSI service itself starts up. This is the typical configuration.

Onboot: This option is used for iSCSI targets that are to be connected during boot; that is, when root (/) is on iSCSI. As such, the iSCSI target device will be evaluated from the initrd on server boots.

Discovered Targets:

The *Discovered Targets* tab provides the possibility of manually discovering iSCSI targets in the network.

13.3.1.1   Configuring the iSCSI Initiator

1. Start YaST and launch *Network Services* > *iSCSI LIO Target.*

2. Switch to the *Services* tab.

3. Under *Service Start*, specify how you want the iSCSI initiator service to be started:

   - **When Booting:** The service starts automatically on server restart.

   - **Manually:** (Default) You must start the service manually after a server restart by running `sudo systemctl start iscsi iscsid`.

4. Specify or verify the *Initiator Name.*

   Specify a well-formed iSCSI qualified name (IQN) for the iSCSI initiator on this server. The initiator name must be globally unique on your network. The IQN uses the following general format:

   ```
   iqn.yyyy-mm.com.mycompany:n1:n2
   ```

   where n1 and n2 are alphanumeric characters. For example:

   ```
   iqn.1996-04.de.suse:01:a5dfcea717a
   ```

The *Initiator Name* is automatically completed with the corresponding value from the `/etc/iscsi/initiatorname.iscsi` file on the server.

If the server has iBFT (iSCSI Boot Firmware Table) support, the *Initiator Name* is completed with the corresponding value in the IBFT, and you are not able to change the initiator name in this interface. Use the BIOS Setup to modify it instead. The iBFT is a block of information containing various parameters useful to the iSCSI boot process, including iSCSI target and initiator descriptions for the server.

5. Use either of the following methods to discover iSCSI targets on the network.

   - **iSNS:** To use iSNS (Internet Storage Name Service) for discovering iSCSI targets, continue with *Section 13.3.1.2, "Discovering iSCSI Targets by Using iSNS"*.

   - **Discovered Targets:** To discover iSCSI target devices manually, continue with *Section 13.3.1.3, "Discovering iSCSI Targets Manually"*.

13.3.1.2   Discovering iSCSI Targets by Using iSNS

Before you can use this option, you must have already installed and configured an iSNS server in your environment. For information, see *Chapter 12, iSNS for Linux*.

1. In YaST, select *iSCSI Initiator,* then select the *Service* tab.

2. Specify the IP address of the iSNS server and port. The default port is 3205.

3. Click *Finish* to save and apply your changes.

13.3.1.3   Discovering iSCSI Targets Manually

Repeat the following process for each of the iSCSI target servers that you want to access from the server where you are setting up the iSCSI initiator.

1. In YaST, select *iSCSI Initiator,* then select the *Discovered Targets* tab.

2. Click *Discovery* to open the iSCSI Initiator Discovery dialog box.

3. Enter the IP address and change the port if needed. The default port is 3260.

4. If authentication is required, deselect *No Authentication,* then specify the credentials for *Incoming* or *Outgoing* authentication.

5. Click *Next* to start the discovery and connect to the iSCSI target server.

6. If credentials are required, after a successful discovery, use *Connect* to activate the target. You are prompted for authentication credentials to use the selected iSCSI target.

7. Click *Next* to finish the configuration.
   The target now appears in *Connected Targets* and the virtual iSCSI device is now available.

8. Click *Finish* to save and apply your changes.

9. You can find the local device path for the iSCSI target device by using the `lsscsi` command.

13.3.1.4   Setting the Start-up Preference for iSCSI Target Devices

1. In YaST, select *iSCSI Initiator,* then select the *Connected Targets* tab to view a list of the iSCSI target devices that are currently connected to the server.

2. Select the iSCSI target device that you want to manage.

3. Click *Toggle Start-Up* to modify the setting:

   Automatic: This option is used for iSCSI targets that are to be connected when the iSCSI service itself starts up. This is the typical configuration.

   Onboot: This option is used for iSCSI targets that are to be connected during boot; that is, when root (/) is on iSCSI. As such, the iSCSI target device will be evaluated from the initrd on server boots.

4. Click *Finish* to save and apply your changes.

13.3.2   Setting Up the iSCSI Initiator Manually

Both the discovery and the configuration of iSCSI connections require a running iscsid. When running the discovery the first time, the internal database of the iSCSI initiator is created in the directory `/etc/iscsi/`.

If your discovery is password protected, provide the authentication information to iscsid. Because the internal database does not exist when doing the first discovery, it cannot be used now. Instead, the configuration file /etc/iscsid.conf must be edited to provide the information. To add your password information for the discovery, add the following lines to the end of /etc/iscsid.conf:

```
discovery.sendtargets.auth.authmethod = CHAP
discovery.sendtargets.auth.username = username
discovery.sendtargets.auth.password = password
```

The discovery stores all received values in an internal persistent database. In addition, it displays all detected targets. Run this discovery with the following command:

```
sudo iscsiadm -m discovery --type=st --portal=target_ip
```

The output should look like the following:

```
10.44.171.99:3260,1 iqn.2006-02.com.example.iserv:systems
```

To discover the available targets on an iSNS server, use the following command:

```
sudo iscsiadm --mode discovery --type isns --portal target_ip
```

For each target defined on the iSCSI target, one line appears. For more information about the stored data, see *Section 13.3.3, "The iSCSI Client Databases"*.

The special --login option of **iscsiadm** creates all needed devices:

```
sudo iscsiadm -m node -n iqn.2006-02.com.example.iserv:systems --login
```

The newly generated devices show up in the output of **lsscsi** and can now be mounted.

13.3.3   The iSCSI Client Databases

All information that was discovered by the iSCSI initiator is stored in two database files that reside in /etc/iscsi. There is one database for the discovery of targets and one for the discovered nodes. When accessing a database, you first must select if you want to get your data from the discovery or from the node database. Do this with the `-m discovery` and `-m node` parameters of **iscsiadm**. Using **iscsiadm** with one of these parameters gives an overview of the stored records:

```
tux > sudo iscsiadm -m discovery
10.44.171.99:3260,1 iqn.2006-02.com.example.iserv:systems
```

The target name in this example is `iqn.2006-02.com.example.iserv:systems`. This name is needed for all actions that relate to this special data set. To examine the content of the data record with the ID `iqn.2006-02.com.example.iserv:systems`, use the following command:

```
tux > sudo iscsiadm -m node --targetname iqn.2006-02.com.example.iserv:systems
node.name = iqn.2006-02.com.example.iserv:systems
node.transport_name = tcp
node.tpgt = 1
node.active_conn = 1
node.startup = manual
node.session.initial_cmdsn = 0
node.session.reopen_max = 32
node.session.auth.authmethod = CHAP
node.session.auth.username = joe
node.session.auth.password = ********
node.session.auth.username_in = empty
node.session.auth.password_in = empty
node.session.timeo.replacement_timeout = 0
node.session.err_timeo.abort_timeout = 10
node.session.err_timeo.reset_timeout = 30
node.session.iscsi.InitialR2T = No
node.session.iscsi.ImmediateData = Yes
....
```

To edit the value of one of these variables, use the command **iscsiadm** with the `update` operation. For example, if you want iscsid to log in to the iSCSI target when it initializes, set the variable `node.startup` to the value `automatic`:

```
sudo iscsiadm -m node -n iqn.2006-02.com.example.iserv:systems \
-p ip:port --op=update --name=node.startup --value=automatic
```

Remove obsolete data sets with the <u>delete</u> operation. If the target `iqn.2006-02.com.example.iserv:systems` is no longer a valid record, delete this record with the following command:

```
sudo iscsiadm -m node -n iqn.2006-02.com.example.iserv:systems \
-p ip:port --op=delete
```

Important: No Confirmation

Use this option with caution because it deletes the record without any additional confirmation prompt.

To get a list of all discovered targets, run the **sudo iscsiadm -m node** command.

13.4 Using iSCSI Disks when Installing

Booting from an iSCSI disk on x86_64 and IBM POWER architectures is supported, when iSCSI-enabled firmware is used.

To use iSCSI disks during installation, it is necessary to add the following parameter to the boot option line:

```
withiscsi=1
```

During installation, an additional screen appears that provides the option to attach iSCSI disks to the system and use them in the installation process.

13.5 Troubleshooting iSCSI

This section describes some known issues and possible solutions for iSCSI target and iSCSI initiator issues.

13.5.1 Portal Error When Setting Up Target LUNs on an iSCSI LIO Target Server

When adding or editing an iSCSI LIO target group, you get an error:

```
Problem setting network portal ip_address:3260
```

The `/var/log/YaST2/y2log` log file contains the following error:

```
find: `/sys/kernel/config/target/iscsi': No such file or directory
```

This problem occurs if the iSCSI LIO Target Server software is not currently running. To resolve this issue, exit YaST, manually start iSCSI LIO at the command line with **systemctl start target**, then try again.

You can also enter the following to check if **configfs**, **iscsi_target_mod**, and **target_core_mod** are loaded. A sample response is shown.

```
tux > sudo lsmod | grep iscsi
iscsi_target_mod        295015  0
target_core_mod         346745  4
iscsi_target_mod,target_core_pscsi,target_core_iblock,target_core_file
configfs                 35817  3 iscsi_target_mod,target_core_mod
scsi_mod                231620  16
iscsi_target_mod,target_core_pscsi,target_core_mod,sg,sr_mod,mptctl,sd_mod,
scsi_dh_rdac,scsi_dh_emc,scsi_dh_alua,scsi_dh_hp_sw,scsi_dh,libata,mptspi,
mptscsih,scsi_transport_spi
```

13.5.2 iSCSI LIO Targets Are Not Visible from Other Computers

If you use a firewall on the target server, you must open the iSCSI port that you are using to allow other computers to see the iSCSI LIO targets. For information, see *Section 13.2.1, "iSCSI LIO Target Service Start-up and Firewall Settings"*.

13.5.3   Data Packets Dropped for iSCSI Traffic

A firewall might drop packets if it gets too busy. The default for the SUSE Firewall is to drop packets after three minutes. If you find that iSCSI traffic packets are being dropped, you can consider configuring the SUSE Firewall to queue packets instead of dropping them when it gets too busy.

13.5.4   Using iSCSI Volumes with LVM

Use the troubleshooting tips in this section when using LVM on iSCSI targets.

13.5.4.1   Check if the iSCSI Initiator Discovery Occurs at Boot

When you set up the iSCSI Initiator, ensure that you enable discovery at boot time so that udev can discover the iSCSI devices at boot time and set up the devices to be used by LVM.

13.5.4.2   Check that iSCSI Target Discovery Occurs at Boot

Remember that udev provides the default setup for devices. Ensure that all of the applications that create devices are started at boot time so that **udev** can recognize and assign devices for them at system start-up. If the application or service is not started until later, **udev** does not create the device automatically as it would at boot time.

13.5.5   iSCSI Targets Are Mounted When the Configuration File Is Set to Manual

When Open-iSCSI starts, it can mount the targets even if the node.startup option is set to manual in the /etc/iscsi/iscsid.conf file if you manually modified the configuration file. Check the /etc/iscsi/nodes/*target_name*/*ip_address,port*/default file. It contains a node.startup setting that overrides the /etc/iscsi/iscsid.conf file. Setting the mount option to manual by using the YaST interface also sets node.startup = manual in the /etc/iscsi/nodes/*target_name*/*ip_address,port*/default files.

13.6 iSCSI LIO Target Terminology

backstore

> A physical storage object that provides the actual storage underlying an iSCSI endpoint.

CDB (command descriptor block)

> The standard format for SCSI commands. CDBs are commonly 6, 10, or 12 bytes long, though they can be 16 bytes or of variable length.

CHAP (Challenge Handshake Authentication Protocol)

> A point-to-point protocol (PPP) authentication method used to confirm the identity of one computer to another. After the Link Control Protocol (LCP) connects the two computers, and the CHAP method is negotiated, the authenticator sends a random Challenge to the peer. The peer issues a cryptographically hashed Response that depends upon the Challenge and a secret key. The authenticator verifies the hashed Response against its own calculation of the expected hash value, and either acknowledges the authentication or terminates the connection. CHAP is defined in the RFC 1994.

CID (connection identifier)

> A 16-bit number, generated by the initiator, that uniquely identifies a connection between two iSCSI devices. This number is presented during the login phase.

endpoint

> The combination of an iSCSI Target Name with an iSCSI TPG (IQN + Tag).

EUI (extended unique identifier)

> A 64-bit number that uniquely identifies every device in the world. The format consists of 24 bits that are unique to a given company, and 40 bits assigned by the company to each device it builds.

initiator

> The originating end of an SCSI session. Typically a controlling device such as a computer.

IPS (Internet Protocol storage)

> The class of protocols or devices that use the IP protocol to move data in a storage network. FCIP (Fibre Channel over Internet Protocol), iFCP (Internet Fibre Channel Protocol), and iSCSI (Internet SCSI) are all examples of IPS protocols.

IQN (iSCSI qualified name)

> A name format for iSCSI that uniquely identifies every device in the world (for example: `iqn.5886.com.acme.tapedrive.sn-a12345678`).

ISID (initiator session identifier)

A 48-bit number, generated by the initiator, that uniquely identifies a session between the initiator and the target. This value is created during the login process, and is sent to the target with a Login PDU.

MCS (multiple connections per session)

A part of the iSCSI specification that allows multiple TCP/IP connections between an initiator and a target.

MPIO (multipath I/O)

A method by which data can take multiple redundant paths between a server and storage.

network portal

The combination of an iSCSI endpoint with an IP address plus a TCP (Transmission Control Protocol) port. TCP port 3260 is the port number for the iSCSI protocol, as defined by IANA (Internet Assigned Numbers Authority).

SAM (SCSI architectural model)

A document that describes the behavior of SCSI in general terms, allowing for different types of devices communicating over various media.

target

The receiving end of an SCSI session, typically a device such as a disk drive, tape drive, or scanner.

target group (TG)

A list of SCSI target ports that are all treated the same when creating views. Creating a view can help simplify LUN (logical unit number) mapping. Each view entry specifies a target group, host group, and a LUN.

target port

The combination of an iSCSI endpoint with one or more LUNs.

target port group (TPG)

A list of IP addresses and TCP port numbers that determines which interfaces a specific iSCSI target will listen to.

target session identifier (TSID)

A 16-bit number, generated by the target, that uniquely identifies a session between the initiator and the target. This value is created during the login process, and is sent to the initiator with a Login Response PDU (protocol data units).

13.7 Additional Information

The iSCSI protocol has been available for several years. There are many reviews comparing iSCSI with SAN solutions, benchmarking performance, and there also is documentation describing hardware solutions. Important pages for more information about open-iscsi are:

- *Open-iSCSI Project* (http://www.open-iscsi.org/)

- *AppNote: iFolder on Open Enterprise Server Linux Cluster using iSCSI* (http://www.novell.com/coolsolutions/appnote/15394.html)

There is also some online documentation available. See the man pages for **iscsiadm**, **iscsid**, `ietd.conf`, and **ietd** and the example configuration file `/etc/iscsid.conf`.

14 Fibre Channel Storage over Ethernet Networks: FCoE

Many enterprise data centers rely on Ethernet for their LAN and data traffic, and on Fibre Channel networks for their storage infrastructure. Open Fibre Channel over Ethernet (FCoE) Initiator software allows servers with Ethernet adapters to connect to a Fibre Channel storage subsystem over an Ethernet network. This connectivity was previously reserved exclusively for systems with Fibre Channel adapters over a Fibre Channel fabric. The FCoE technology reduces complexity in the data center by aiding network convergence. This helps to preserve your existing investments in a Fibre Channel storage infrastructure and to simplify network management.

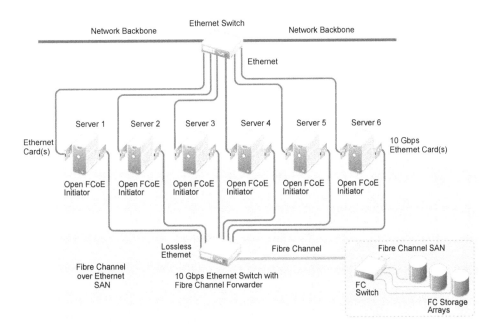

FIGURE 14.1: OPEN FIBRE CHANNEL OVER ETHERNET SAN

Open-FCoE allows you to run the Fibre Channel protocols on the host, instead of on proprietary hardware on the host bus adapter. It is targeted for 10 Gbps (gigabit per second) Ethernet adapters, but can work on any Ethernet adapter that supports pause frames. The initiator software provides a Fibre Channel protocol processing module and an Ethernet-based transport module. The Open-FCoE module acts as a low-level driver for SCSI. The Open-FCoE transport uses **net_device** to send and receive packets. Data Center Bridging (DCB) drivers provide the quality of service for FCoE.

FCoE is an encapsulation protocol that moves the Fibre Channel protocol traffic over Ethernet connections without changing the Fibre Channel frame. This allows your network security and traffic management infrastructure to work the same with FCoE as it does with Fibre Channel.

You might choose to deploy FCoE in your enterprise if the following conditions exist:

- Your enterprise already has a Fibre Channel storage subsystem and administrators with Fibre Channel skills and knowledge.

- You are deploying 10 Gbps Ethernet in the network.

This section describes how to set up FCoE in your network.

14.1 Configuring FCoE Interfaces during the Installation

The YaST installation for SUSE Linux Enterprise Server allows you to configure FCoE disks during the operating system installation if FCoE is enabled at the switch for the connections between the server and the Fibre Channel storage infrastructure. Some system BIOS types can automatically detect the FCoE disks, and report the disks to the YaST Installation software. However, automatic detection of FCoE disks is not supported by all BIOS types. To enable automatic detection in this case, you can add the `withfcoe` option to the kernel command line when you begin the installation:

```
withfcoe=1
```

When the FCoE disks are detected, the YaST installation offers the option to configure FCoE instances at that time. On the Disk Activation page, select *Configure FCoE Interfaces* to access the FCoE configuration. For information about configuring the FCoE interfaces, see *Section 14.3, "Managing FCoE Services with YaST"*.

14.2   Installing FCoE and the YaST FCoE Client

You can set up FCoE disks in your storage infrastructure by enabling FCoE at the switch for the connections to a server. If FCoE disks are available when the SUSE Linux Enterprise Server operating system is installed, the FCoE Initiator software is automatically installed at that time.

If the FCoE Initiator software and the YaST FCoE Client software are not installed, use the following procedure to manually install them with the following command:

```
sudo zypper in yast2-fcoe-client fcoe-utils
```

Alternatively, use the YaST Software Manager to install the packages listed above.

14.3   Managing FCoE Services with YaST

You can use the YaST FCoE Client Configuration option to create, configure, and remove FCoE interfaces for the FCoE disks in your Fibre Channel storage infrastructure. To use this option, the FCoE Initiator service (the `fcoemon` daemon) and the Link Layer Discovery Protocol agent daemon (`llpad`) must be installed and running, and the FCoE connections must be enabled at the FCoE-capable switch.

1. Launch YaST and select *Network Services* ⟩ *FCoE Client Configuration*.

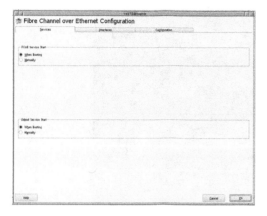

2. On the *Services* tab, view or modify the FCoE service and Lldpad (Link Layer Discovery Protocol agent daemon) service start time as necessary.

    - **FCoE Service Start:** Specifies whether to start the Fibre Channel over Ethernet service `fcoemon` daemon at the server boot time or manually. The daemon controls the FCoE interfaces and establishes a connection with the `llpad` daemon. The values are *When Booting* (default) or *Manually*.

    - **Lldpad Service Start:** Specifies whether to start the Link Layer Discovery Protocol agent `llpad` daemon at the server boot time or manually. The `llpad` daemon informs the `fcoemon` daemon about the Data Center Bridging features and the configuration of the FCoE interfaces. The values are *When Booting* (default) or *Manually*.

    If you modify a setting, click *OK* to save and apply the change.

3. On the *Interfaces* tab, view information about all of the detected network adapters on the server, including information about VLAN and FCoE configuration. You can also create an FCoE VLAN interface, change settings for an existing FCoE interface, or remove an FCoE interface.

Use the *FCoE VLAN Interface* column to determine whether FCoE is available or not:

Interface Name

> If a name is assigned to the interface, such as `eth4.200`, FCoE is available on the switch, and the FCoE interface is activated for the adapter.

Not Configured:

> If the status is *not configured*, FCoE is enabled on the switch, but an FCoE interface has not been activated for the adapter. Select the adapter, then click *Create FCoE VLAN Interface* to activate the interface on the adapter.

Not Available:

> If the status is *not available*, FCoE is not possible for the adapter because FCoE has not been enabled for that connection on the switch.

4. To set up an FCoE-enabled adapter that has not yet been configured, select it and click *Create FCoE VLAN Interface*. Confirm the query with *Yes*.

   The adapter is now listed with an interface name in the *FCoE VLAN Interface* column.

5. To change the settings for an adapter that is already configured, select it from the list, then click *Change Settings*.

   The following options can be configured:

FCoE Enable

> Enable or disable the creation of FCoE instances for the adapter.

DCB Required

> Specifies whether Data Center Bridging is required for the adapter (usually this is the case).

Auto VLAN

Specifies whether the `fcoemon` daemon creates the VLAN interfaces automatically.

If you modify a setting, click *Next* to save and apply the change. The settings are written to the `/etc/fcoe/ethX` file. The `fcoemon` daemon reads the configuration files for each FCoE interface when it is initialized.

6. To remove an interface that is already configured, select it from the list. Click *Remove Interface* and *Continue* to confirm. The FCoE Interface value changes to *not configured*.

7. On the *Configuration* tab, view or modify the general settings for the FCoE system service. You can enable or disable debugging messages from the FCoE service script and the `fcoemon` daemon and specify whether messages are sent to the system log.

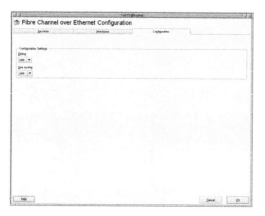

8. Click *OK* to save and apply changes.

14.4   Configuring FCoE with Commands

1. Open a terminal console.

2. Use YaST to configure the Ethernet network interface card, such as `eth2`.

3. Start the Link Layer Discovery Protocol agent daemon (`llpad`).

```
sudo systemctl start lldpad
```

4. Enable Data Center Bridging on your Ethernet adapter.

```
tux > dcbtool sc eth2 dcb on
  Version:      2
  Command:      Set Config
  Feature:      DCB State
  Port:         eth2
  Status:       Successful
```

5. Enable and set the Priority Flow Control (PFC) settings for Data Center Bridging.

```
sudo dcbtool sc eth<x> pfc e:1 a:1 w:1
```

Argument setting values are:

e:<0|1>

Controls feature enablement.

a:<0|1>

Controls whether the feature is advertised via Data Center Bridging Exchange protocol to the peer.

w:<0|1>

Controls whether the feature is willing to change its operational configuration based on what is received from the peer.

6. Enable the Data Center Bridging to accept the switch's priority setting for FCoE.

```
tux > sudo dcbtool sc eth2 app:fcoe e:1
  Version:      2
  Command:      Set Config
  Feature:      Application FCoE
  Port:         eth2
  Status:       Successful
```

7. Copy the default FCoE configuration file to `/etc/fcoe/cfg-eth2`.

```
sudo cp /etc/fcoe/cfg-ethx /etc/fcoe/cfg-eth2
```

8. Start the FCoE Initiator service.

```
systemctl start fcoe.status
```

9. Set up the Link Layer Discovery Protocol agent daemon (`llpad`) and the FCoE Initiator service to start when booting.

```
systemctl enable llpad fcoe
```

14.5 Managing FCoE Instances with the FCoE Administration Tool

The **fcoeadm** utility is the Fibre Channel over Ethernet (FCoE) management tool. It can be used to create, destroy, and reset an FCoE instance on a given network interface. The **fcoeadm** utility sends commands to a running `fcoemon` process via a socket interface. For information about **fcoemon**, see the `man 8 fcoemon`.

The **fcoeadm** utility allows you to query the FCoE instances about the following:

- Interfaces

- Target LUNs

- Port statistics

The **fcoeadm** utility is part of the `fcoe-utils` package. The general syntax for the command looks like the following:

```
fcoeadm
  [-c|--create] [<ethX>]
  [-d|--destroy] [<ethX>]
  [-r|--reset] [<ethX>]
  [-S|--Scan] [<ethX>]
  [-i|--interface] [<ethX>]
  [-t|--target] [<ethX>]
  [-l|--lun] [<ethX>]
  [-s|--stats <ethX>] [<interval>]
  [-v|--version]
```

```
[-h|--help]
```

Refer to **man 8 fcoeadm** for details.

Examples

fcoeadm -c eth2.101

Create an FCoE instance on eth2.101.

fcoeadm -d eth2.101

Destroy an FCoE instance on eth2.101.

fcoeadm -i eth3

Show information about all of the FCoE instances on interface eth3. If no interface is specified, information for all interfaces that have FCoE instances created will be shown. The following example shows information on connection eth0.201:

```
tux > sudo fcoeadm -i eth0.201
  Description:      82599EB 10-Gigabit SFI/SFP+ Network Connection
  Revision:        01
  Manufacturer:    Intel Corporation
  Serial Number:   001B219B258C
  Driver:          ixgbe 3.3.8-k2
  Number of Ports: 1

      Symbolic Name:     fcoe v0.1 over eth0.201
      OS Device Name:    host8
      Node Name:         0x1000001B219B258E
      Port Name:         0x2000001B219B258E
      FabricName:        0x2001000573D38141
      Speed:             10 Gbit
      Supported Speed:   10 Gbit
      MaxFrameSize:      2112
      FC-ID (Port ID):   0x790003
      State:             Online
```

fcoeadm -l eth3.101

Show detailed information about all of the LUNs discovered on connection eth3.101. If no connection is specified, information about all of the LUNs discovered on all FCoE connections will be shown.

fcoeadm -r eth2.101

Reset the FCoE instance on eth2.101.

fcoeadm -s eth3 3

Show statistical information about a specific eth3 port that has FCoE instances, at an interval of three seconds. The statistics are displayed one line per time interval. If no interval is given, the default of one second is used.

fcoeadm -t eth3

Show information about all of the discovered targets from a given eth3 port having FCoE instances. After each discovered target, any associated LUNs are listed. If no instance is specified, targets from all of the ports that have FCoE instances are shown. The following example shows information of targets from the eth0.201 connection:

```
tux > sudo fcoeadm -t eth0.201
  Interface:        eth0.201
  Roles:            FCP Target
  Node Name:        0x200000D0231B5C72
  Port Name:        0x210000D0231B5C72
  Target ID:        0
  MaxFrameSize:     2048
  OS Device Name:   rport-8:0-7
  FC-ID (Port ID):  0x79000C
  State:            Online

LUN ID  Device Name  Capacity  Block Size  Description
------  -----------  --------  ----------  ---------------------------
    40  /dev/sdqi    792.84 GB        512  IFT DS S24F-R2840-4 (rev 386C)
    72  /dev/sdpk    650.00 GB        512  IFT DS S24F-R2840-4 (rev 386C)
   168  /dev/sdgy      1.30 TB        512  IFT DS S24F-R2840-4 (rev 386C)
```

14.6 Additional Information

For information, see the follow documentation:

- For information about the Open-FCoE service daemon, see the `fcoemon(8)` man page.

- For information about the Open-FCoE Administration tool, see the `fcoeadm(8)` man page.

- For information about the Data Center Bridging Configuration tool, see the `dcbtool(8)` man page.

- For information about the Link Layer Discovery Protocol agent daemon, see the `lld-pad(8)` man page.

- For general information, see the Open-FCoE home page: http://www.open-fcoe.org/dokuwiki/start.

15 Managing Multipath I/O for Devices

This section describes how to manage failover and path load balancing for multiple paths between the servers and block storage devices by using Multipath I/O (MPIO).

15.1 Understanding Multipath I/O

Multipathing is the ability of a server to communicate with the same physical or logical block storage device across multiple physical paths between the host bus adapters in the server and the storage controllers for the device, typically in Fibre Channel (FC) or iSCSI SAN environments. You can also achieve multiple connections with direct attached storage when multiple channels are available.

Linux multipathing provides connection fault tolerance and can provide load balancing across the active connections. When multipathing is configured and running, it automatically isolates and identifies device connection failures, and reroutes I/O to alternate connections.

Typical connection problems involve faulty adapters, cables, or controllers. When you configure multipath I/O for a device, the multipath driver monitors the active connection between devices. When the multipath driver detects I/O errors for an active path, it fails over the traffic to the device's designated secondary path. When the preferred path becomes healthy again, control can be returned to the preferred path.

15.2 Hardware Support

The multipathing drivers and tools support all architectures for which SUSE Linux Enterprise Server is available. They support most storage arrays. The storage array that houses the multipathed device must support multipathing to use the multipathing drivers and tools. Some storage array vendors provide their own multipathing management tools. Consult the vendor's hardware documentation to determine what settings are required.

15.2.1 Storage Arrays That Are Automatically Detected for Multipathing

The `multipath-tools` package automatically detects the following storage arrays:

3PARdata VV

AIX NVDISK

AIX VDASD

APPLE Xserve RAID

COMPELNT Compellent Vol

COMPAQ/HP HSV101, HSV111, HSV200, HSV210, HSV300, HSV400, HSV 450

COMPAQ/HP MSA, HSV

COMPAQ/HP MSA VOLUME

DataCore SANmelody

DDN SAN DataDirector

DEC HSG80

DELL MD3000

DELL MD3000i

DELL MD32xx

DELL MD32xxi

DGC

EMC Clariion

EMC Invista

EMC SYMMETRIX

EUROLOGC FC2502

FSC CentricStor

FUJITSU ETERNUS_DX, DXL, DX400, DX8000

HITACHI DF

HITACHI/HP OPEN

HP A6189A

HP HSVX700

HP LOGICAL VOLUME

HP MSA2012fc, MSA 2212fc, MSA2012i

HP MSA2012sa, MSA2312 fc/i/sa, MCA2324 fc/i/sa, MSA2000s VOLUME

HP P2000 G3 FC|P2000G3 FC/iSCSI|P2000 G3 SAS|P2000 G3 iSCSI

IBM 1722-600

IBM 1724

IBM 1726

IBM 1742

IBM 1745, 1746

IBM 1750500

IBM 1814

IBM 1815

IBM 1818

IBM 1820N00

IBM 2105800

IBM 2105F20

IBM 2107900

IBM 2145

IBM 2810XIV

IBM 3303 NVDISK

IBM 3526

IBM 3542

IBM IPR

IBM Nseries

IBM ProFibre 4000R

IBM S/390 DASD ECKD

IBM S/390 DASD FBA

Intel Multi-Flex

LSI/ENGENIO INF-01-00

NEC DISK ARRAY

NETAPP LUN

NEXENTA COMSTAR

Pillar Axiom

PIVOT3 RAIGE VOLUME

SGI IS

SGI TP9100, TP 9300

SGI TP9400, TP9500

STK FLEXLINE 380

STK OPENstorage D280

SUN CSM200_R

SUN LCSM100_[IEFS]

SUN STK6580, STK6780

SUN StorEdge 3510, T4

SUN SUN_6180

In general, most other storage arrays should work. When storage arrays are automatically detected, the default settings for multipathing apply. If you want non-default settings, you must manually create and configure the `/etc/multipath.conf` file. The same applies for hardware that is not automatically detected. For information, see *Section 15.6, "Creating or Modifying the /etc/multipath.conf File"*.

Consider the following caveats:

- Not all of the storage arrays that are automatically detected have been tested on SUSE Linux Enterprise Server. Also see *Section 15.2.2, "Tested Storage Arrays for Multipathing Support"*.

- Some storage arrays might require specific hardware handlers. A hardware handler is a kernel module that performs hardware-specific actions when switching path groups and dealing with I/O errors. For information, see *Section 15.2.3, "Storage Arrays that Require Specific Hardware Handlers"*.

- After you modify the `/etc/multipath.conf` file, you must run **dracut** `-f` to re-create the `initrd` on your system, then reboot in order for the changes to take effect.

15.2.2   Tested Storage Arrays for Multipathing Support

Storage arrays from the following vendors have been tested with SUSE Linux Enterprise Server:

EMC
Hitachi
Hewlett-Packard/Compaq
IBM
NetApp
SGI

Most other vendor storage arrays should also work. Consult your vendor's documentation for guidance. For a list of the default storage arrays recognized by the `multipath-tools` package, see *Section 15.2.1, "Storage Arrays That Are Automatically Detected for Multipathing"*.

15.2.3 Storage Arrays that Require Specific Hardware Handlers

Storage arrays that require special commands on failover from one path to the other or that require special nonstandard error handling might require more extensive support. Therefore, the Device Mapper Multipath service has hooks for hardware handlers. For example, one such handler for the EMC CLARiiON CX family of arrays is already provided.

 Important: For More Information

Consult the hardware vendor's documentation to determine if its hardware handler must be installed for Device Mapper Multipath.

The `multipath -t` command shows an internal table of storage arrays that require special handling with specific hardware handlers. The displayed list is not an exhaustive list of supported storage arrays. It lists only those arrays that require special handling and that the `multipath-tools` developers had access to during the tool development.

 Important: Exceptions

Arrays with true active/active multipath support do not require special handling, so they are not listed for the `multipath -t` command.

A listing in the `multipath -t` table does not necessarily mean that SUSE Linux Enterprise Server was tested on that specific hardware. For a list of tested storage arrays, see *Section 15.2.2, "Tested Storage Arrays for Multipathing Support"*.

15.3 Planning for Multipathing

Use the guidelines in this section when planning your multipath I/O solution.

15.3.1   Prerequisites

- Multipathing is managed at the device level.

- The storage array you use for the multipathed device must support multipathing. For more information, see *Section 15.2, "Hardware Support"*.

- You need to configure multipathing only if multiple physical paths exist between host bus adapters in the server and host bus controllers for the block storage device. You configure multipathing for the logical device as seen by the server.

- For some storage arrays, the vendor provides its own multipathing software to manage multipathing for the array's physical and logical devices. In this case, you should follow the vendor's instructions for configuring multipathing for those devices.

- When using multipathing in a virtualization environment, the multipathing is controlled in the host server environment. Configure multipathing for the device before you assign it to a virtual guest machine.

15.3.2   Disk Management Tasks

Perform the following disk management tasks before you attempt to configure multipathing for a physical or logical device that has multiple paths:

- Use third-party tools to carve physical disks into smaller logical disks.

- Use third-party tools to partition physical or logical disks. If you change the partitioning in the running system, the Device Mapper Multipath (DM-MP) module does not automatically detect and reflect these changes. DM-MPIO must be re-initialized, which usually requires a reboot.

- Use third-party SAN array management tools to create and configure hardware RAID devices.

- Use third-party SAN array management tools to create logical devices such as LUNs. Logical device types that are supported for a given array depend on the array vendor.

15.3.3 Volume Managers

Volume managers such as LVM2 and Clustered LVM2 run on top of multipathing. You must configure multipathing for a device before you use LVM2 or cLVM2 to create segment managers and file systems on it. For information, see *Section 15.12, "Using LVM2 on Multipath Devices"*.

15.3.4 Software RAIDs

The Linux software RAID management software runs on top of multipathing. For each device that has multiple I/O paths and that you plan to use in a software RAID, you must configure the device for multipathing before you attempt to create the software RAID device. Automatic discovery of multipathed devices is not available. The software RAID is not aware of the multipathing management running underneath.

For information about setting up multipathing for existing software RAIDs, see *Section 15.13, "Configuring Multipath I/O for an Existing Software RAID"*.

15.3.5 High-Availability Solutions

High-availability solutions for clustering storage resources run on top of the multipathing service on each node. Ensure that the configuration settings in the `/etc/multipath.conf` file on each node are consistent across the cluster.

Ensure that multipath devices have the same name across all devices. Refer to *Section 15.9.1, "Multipath Device Names in HA Clusters"* for details.

The Distributed Replicated Block Device (DRBD) high-availability solution for mirroring devices across a LAN runs on top of multipathing. For each device that has multiple I/O paths and that you plan to use in a DRDB solution, you must configure the device for multipathing before you configure DRBD.

15.4 Multipath Management Tools

The multipathing support in SUSE Linux Enterprise Server is based on the Device Mapper Multipath module of the Linux kernel and the `multipath-tools` userspace package. You can use the Multiple Devices Administration utility (MDADM, **mdadm**) to view the status of multipathed devices.

15.4.1 Device Mapper Multipath Module

The Device Mapper Multipath (DM-MP) module provides the multipathing capability for Linux. DM-MPIO is the preferred solution for multipathing on SUSE Linux Enterprise Server. It is the only multipathing option shipped with the product that is completely supported by SUSE.

DM-MPIO features automatic configuration of the multipathing subsystem for a large variety of setups. Configurations of up to eight paths to each device are supported. Configurations are supported for active/passive (one path active, others passive) or active/active (all paths active with round-robin load balancing).

The DM-MPIO framework is extensible in two ways:

* Using specific hardware handlers. For information, see *Section 15.2.3, "Storage Arrays that Require Specific Hardware Handlers"*.

* Using load-balancing algorithms that are more sophisticated than the round-robin algorithm

The userspace component of DM-MPIO takes care of automatic path discovery and grouping, and automated path retesting, so that a previously failed path is automatically reinstated when it becomes healthy again. This minimizes the need for administrator attention in a production environment.

DM-MPIO protects against failures in the paths to the device, and not failures in the device itself. If one of the active paths is lost (for example, a network adapter breaks or a fiber-optic cable is removed), I/O is redirected to the remaining paths. If the configuration is active/passive, then the path fails over to one of the passive paths. If you are using the round-robin load-balancing configuration, the traffic is balanced across the remaining healthy paths. If all active paths fail, inactive secondary paths must be woken up, so failover occurs with a delay of approximately 30 seconds.

If a disk array has more than one storage processor, ensure that the SAN switch has a connection to the storage processor that owns the LUNs you want to access. On most disk arrays, all LUNs belong to both storage processors, so both connections are active.

Note: Storage Processors

On some disk arrays, the storage array manages the traffic through storage processors so that it presents only one storage processor at a time. One processor is active and the other one is passive until there is a failure. If you are connected to the wrong storage processor (the one with the passive path) you might not see the expected LUNs, or you might see the LUNs but get errors when you try to access them.

TABLE 15.1: MULTIPATH I/O FEATURES OF STORAGE ARRAYS

Features of Storage Arrays	Description
Active/passive controllers	One controller is active and serves all LUNs. The second controller acts as a standby. The second controller also presents the LUNs to the multipath component so that the operating system knows about redundant paths. If the primary controller fails, the second controller takes over, and it serves all LUNs. In some arrays, the LUNs can be assigned to different controllers. A given LUN is assigned to one controller to be its active controller. One controller does the disk I/O for any LUN at a time, and the second controller is the standby for that LUN. The second controller also presents the paths, but disk I/O is not possible. Servers that use that LUN are connected to the LUN's assigned controller. If the primary controller for a set of LUNs fails, the second controller takes over, and it serves all LUNs.
Active/active controllers	Both controllers share the load for all LUNs, and can process disk I/O for any LUN. If one controller fails, the second controller automatically handles all traffic.
Load balancing	The Device Mapper Multipath driver automatically load balances traffic across all active paths.

Device Mapper Multipath Module

Features of Storage Arrays	Description
Controller failover	When the active controller fails over to the passive, or standby, controller, the Device Mapper Multipath driver automatically activates the paths between the host and the standby, making them the primary paths.
Boot/Root device support	Multipathing is supported for the root (/) device in SUSE Linux Enterprise Server 10 and later. The host server must be connected to the currently active controller and storage processor for the boot device. Multipathing is supported for the /boot device in SUSE Linux Enterprise Server 11 and later.

Device Mapper Multipath detects every path for a multipathed device as a separate SCSI device. The SCSI device names take the form /dev/sd*N*, where *N* is an autogenerated letter for the device, beginning with a and issued sequentially as the devices are created, such as /dev/sda, /dev/sdb, and so on. If the number of devices exceeds 26, the letters are duplicated so that the next device after /dev/sdz will be named /dev/sdaa, /dev/sdab, and so on.

If multiple paths are not automatically detected, you can configure them manually in the /etc/multipath.conf file. The multipath.conf file does not exist until you create and configure it. For information, see *Section 15.6, "Creating or Modifying the /etc/multipath.conf File"*.

15.4.2 Multipath I/O Management Tools

The packages multipath-tools and kpartx provide tools that take care of automatic path discovery and grouping. They automatically test the path periodically, so that a previously failed path is automatically reinstated when it becomes healthy again. This minimizes the need for administrator attention in a production environment.

TABLE 15.2: TOOLS IN THE MULTIPATH-TOOLS PACKAGE

Tool	Description
multipath	Scans the system for multipathed devices and assembles them.
multipathd	Waits for maps events, then executes multipath.

Multipath I/O Management Tools

Tool	Description
kpartx	Maps linear devmaps to partitions on the multipathed device, which makes it possible to create multipath monitoring for partitions on the device.
mpathpersist	Manages SCSI-persistent reservations on Device Mapper Multipath devices.ppc

15.4.3 Using MDADM for Multipathed Devices

Udev is the default device handler, and devices are automatically known to the system by the Worldwide ID instead of by the device node name. This resolves problems in previous releases of MDADM and LVM where the configuration files (`mdadm.conf` and `lvm.conf`) did not properly recognize multipathed devices.

As with LVM2, MDADM requires that the devices be accessed by the ID rather than by the device node path. Therefore, the DEVICE entry in /etc/mdadm.conf should be set as follows:

```
DEVICE /dev/disk/by-id/*
```

If you are using user-friendly names, specify the path as follows so that only the device mapper names are scanned after multipathing is configured:

```
DEVICE /dev/disk/by-id/dm-uuid-.*-mpath-.*
```

15.4.4 The multipath Command

Use the Linux **multipath(8)** command to configure and manage multipathed devices. The general syntax for the command looks like the following:

```
multipath [-v verbosity_level] [-b bindings_file] [-d] [-h|-l|-ll|-f|-F|-B|-c|-q|-
r|-w|-W] [-p failover|multibus|group_by_serial|group_by_prio|group_by_node_name]
 [devicename]
```

Refer to **man 8 multipath** for details.

multipath

Configures all multipath devices.

multipath *devicename*

Configures a specific multipath device.

Replace *devicename* with the device node name such as `/dev/sdb` (as shown by udev in the $DEVNAME variable), or in the `major:minor` format. The device may alternatively be a multipath map name.

multipath -f

Selectively suppresses a multipath map, and its device-mapped partitions.

multipath -d

Dry run. Displays potential multipath devices, but does not create any devices and does not update device maps.

multipath -v2 -d

Displays multipath map information for potential multipath devices in a dry run. The -v2 option shows only local disks. This verbosity level prints the created or updated multipath names only for use to feed other tools like kpartx.

There is no output if the device already exists and there are no changes. Use `multipath -ll` to see the status of configured multipath devices.

multipath -v2 *devicename*

Configures a specific potential multipath device and displays multipath map information for it. This verbosity level prints only the created or updated multipath names for use to feed other tools like `kpartx`.

There is no output if the device already exists and there are no changes. Use `multipath -ll` to see the status of configured multipath devices.

Replace *devicename* with the device node name such as `/dev/sdb` (as shown by **udev** in the $DEVNAME variable), or in the `major:minor` format. The device may alternatively be a multipath map name.

multipath -v3

Configures potential multipath devices and displays multipath map information for them. This verbosity level prints all detected paths, multipaths, and device maps. Both wwid and devnode blacklisted devices are displayed.

multipath -v3 *devicename*

Configures a specific potential multipath device and displays information for it. The -v3 option shows the full path list. This verbosity level prints all detected paths, multipaths, and device maps. Both wwid and devnode blacklisted devices are displayed.

Replace *devicename* with the device node name such as `/dev/sdb` (as shown by **udev** in the $DEVNAME variable), or in the `major:minor` format. The device may alternatively be a multipath map name.

multipath -ll

Displays the status of all multipath devices.

multipath -ll *devicename*

Displays the status of a specified multipath device.

Replace *devicename* with the device node name such as `/dev/sdb` (as shown by **udev** in the $DEVNAME variable), or in the `major:minor` format. The device may alternatively be a multipath map name.

multipath -F

Flushes all unused multipath device maps. This unresolves the multiple paths; it does not delete the devices.

multipath -F *devicename*

Flushes unused multipath device maps for a specified multipath device. This unresolves the multiple paths; it does not delete the device.

Replace *devicename* with the device node name such as `/dev/sdb` (as shown by **udev** in the $DEVNAME variable), or in the `major:minor` format. The device may alternatively be a multipath map name.

multipath -p [failover | multibus | group_by_serial | group_by_prio | group_by_node_name]

Sets the group policy by specifying one of the group policy options that are described in the following table:

TABLE 15.3: GROUP POLICY OPTIONS FOR THE MULTIPATH -P COMMAND

Policy Option	Description
failover	(Default) One path per priority group. You can use only one path at a time.
multibus	All paths in one priority group.

Policy Option	Description
group_by_serial	One priority group per detected SCSI serial number (the controller node worldwide number).
group_by_prio	One priority group per path priority value. Paths with the same priority are in the same priority group. Priorities are determined by callout programs specified as a global, per-controller, or per-multipath option in the `/etc/multipath.conf` configuration file.
group_by_node_name	One priority group per target node name. Target node names are fetched in the `/sys/class/fc_transport/target*/node_name` location.

15.4.5   The mpathpersist Utility

The **mpathpersist** utility can be used to manage SCSI persistent reservations on Device Mapper Multipath devices. The general syntax for the command looks like the following:

```
mpathpersist [options] [device]
```

Refer to **man 8 mpathpersist** for details.

Use this utility with the service action reservation key (`reservation_key` attribute) in the `/etc/multipath.conf` file to set persistent reservations for SCSI devices. The attribute is not used by default. If it is not set, the **multipathd** daemon does not check for persistent reservation for newly discovered paths or reinstated paths.

```
reservation_key <reservation key>
```

You can add the attribute to the `defaults` section or the `multipaths` section. For example:

```
multipaths {
  multipath {
    wwid    XXXXXXXXXXXXXXXX
    alias       yellow
    reservation_key  0x123abc
```

```
  }
}
```

Set the `reservation_key` parameter for all mpath devices applicable for persistent management, then restart the `multipathd` daemon by running the following command:

```
sudo systemctl restart multipathd
```

After it is set up, you can specify the reservation key in the **mpathpersist** commands.

Examples

mpathpersist --out --register --param-sark=123abc --prout-type=5 -d /dev/mapper/mpath9
> Register the Service Action Reservation Key for the `/dev/mapper/mpath9` device.

mpathpersisst -i -k -d /dev/mapper/mpath9
> Read the Service Action Reservation Key for the `/dev/mapper/mpath9` device.

mpathpersist --out --reserve --param-sark=123abc --prout-type=8 -d /dev/mapper/mpath9
> Reserve the Service Action Reservation Key for the `/dev/mapper/mpath9` device.

mpathpersist -i -s -d /dev/mapper/mpath9
> Read the reservation status of the `/dev/mapper/mpath9` device.

15.5   Configuring the System for Multipathing

15.5.1   Enabling and Starting Multipath I/O Services

To enable multipath services to start at boot time, run the following command:

```
sudo systemctl enable multipathd
```

To manually start and stop the service in the running system or to check its status, enter one
of the following commands:

```
sudo systemctl start multipathd
```

Configuring the System for Multipathing

```
sudo systemctl stop multipathd
sudo systemctl status multipathd
```

15.5.2   Preparing SAN Devices for Multipathing

Before configuring multipath I/O for your SAN devices, prepare the SAN devices, as necessary, by doing the following:

- Configure and zone the SAN with the vendor's tools.

- Configure permissions for host LUNs on the storage arrays with the vendor's tools.

- Install the Linux HBA driver module. Upon module installation, the driver automatically scans the HBA to discover any SAN devices that have permissions for the host. It presents them to the host for further configuration.

   Note: No Native Multipathing

  Ensure that the HBA driver you are using does not have native multipathing enabled.

  See the vendor's specific instructions for more details.

- After the driver module is loaded, discover the device nodes assigned to specific array LUNs or partitions.

- If the SAN device will be used as the root device on the server, modify the timeout settings for the device as described in *Section 15.14.9, "SAN Timeout Settings When the Root Device Is Multipathed"*.

If the LUNs are not seen by the HBA driver, `lsscsi` can be used to check whether the SCSI devices are seen correctly by the operating system. When the LUNs are not seen by the HBA driver, check the zoning setup of the SAN. In particular, check whether LUN masking is active and whether the LUNs are correctly assigned to the server.

If the LUNs are seen by the HBA driver, but there are no corresponding block devices, additional kernel parameters are needed to change the SCSI device scanning behavior, such as to indicate that LUNs are not numbered consecutively. For information, see *TID 3955167: Troubleshooting SCSI (LUN) Scanning Issues* in the SUSE Knowledgebase at https://www.suse.com/support/kb/doc.php?id=3955167.

15.5.3   Partitioning Multipath Devices

Partitioning devices that have multiple paths is not recommended, but it is supported. You can use the **kpartx** tool to create partitions on multipath devices without rebooting. You can also partition the device before you attempt to configure multipathing by using the Partitioner function in YaST, or by using a third-party partitioning tool.

Multipath devices are device-mapper devices. Modifying device-mapper devices with command line tools (such as parted, kpartx, or fdisk) works, but it does not necessarily generate the udev events that are required to update other layers. After you partition the device-mapper device, you should check the multipath map to make sure the device-mapper devices were mapped. If they are missing, you can remap the multipath devices or reboot the server to pick up all of the new partitions in the multipath map.

The device-mapper device for a partition on a multipath device is not the same as an independent device. When you create an LVM logical volume using the whole device, you must specify a device that contains no partitions. If you specify a multipath partition as the target device for the LVM logical volume, LVM recognizes that the underlying physical device is partitioned and the create fails. If you need to subdivide a SAN device, you can carve LUNs on the SAN device and present each LUN as a separate multipath device to the server.

15.5.4   Configuring the Device Drivers in initrd for Multipathing

The server must be manually configured to automatically load the device drivers for the controllers to which the multipath I/O devices are connected within the `initrd`. You need to add the necessary driver module to the variable `force_drivers` in the file `/etc/dracut.conf.d/01-dist.conf`.

For example, if your system contains a RAID controller accessed by the `hpsa` driver and multipathed devices connected to a QLogic controller accessed by the driver qla23xx, this entry would look like:

```
force_drivers+="hpsa qla23xx"
```

After changing `/etc/dracut.conf.d/01-dist.conf`, you must re-create the `initrd` on your system with the **dracut** `-f` command, then reboot in order for the changes to take effect.

There are four SCSI hardware handlers available in the SCSI layer that can be used with DM-Multipath:

```
scsi_dh_alua
scsi_dh_rdac
scsi_dh_hp_sw
scsi_dh_emc
```

Add the modules to the `initrd` image, then specify them in the `/etc/multipath.conf` file as hardware handler types `alua`, `rdac`, `hp_sw`, and `emc`. For example, add one of these lines for a device definition:

```
hardware_handler "1 alua"
hardware_handler "1 rdac"
hardware_handler "1 hp_sw"
hardware_handler "1 emc"
```

To include the modules in the `initrd` image:

1. Add the device handler modules to the `force_drivers` variable in `/etc/dracut.conf.d/01-dist.conf`:

   ```
   force_drivers+="alua rdac hp_sw emc"
   ```

2. Create a new `initrd`:

   ```
   sudo dracut /boot/initrd-kernelversion-scsi-dh \
   kernelversion
   ```

   Replace `kernelversion` with the version of the Kernel you want to use for the initrd, for example:

   ```
   sudo dracut /boot/initrd-3.12.28-4-default-scsi-dh 3.12.28-4-default
   ```

3. Make the initrd generated in the previous step the default initrd that is used for booting:

   ```
   cd /boot && sudo ln -sf initrd-kernelversion-scsi-dh initrd
   ```

For example:

```
cd /boot && sudo ln -sf initrd-3.12.28-4-default-scsi-dh initrd
```

4. Restart the server.

15.6   Creating or Modifying the /etc/multipath.conf File

The `/etc/multipath.conf` file does not exist unless you create it. Default multipath device settings are applied automatically when the **multipathd** daemon runs unless you create the multipath configuration file and personalize the settings. The `/usr/share/doc/packages/multipath-tools/` file contains sample `/etc/multipath.conf` files that you can use as a template.

> **Important: Permanently Applying Changes from** `/etc/multipath.conf`
>
> Whenever you create or modify `/etc/multipath.conf` changes are not permanently applied by just saving the file. Follow the instructions in *Section 15.6.4, "Applying the /etc/multipath.conf File Changes to Update the Multipath Maps"* to apply them and to update the multipath maps.

Whenever you create or modify the `/etc/multipath.conf` file, the changes are not automatically applied when you save the file. This allows you time to perform a dry run to verify your changes before they are committed. When you are satisfied with the revised settings, you can update the multipath maps for the running `multipathd` daemon to use, or the changes will be applied the next time that the `multipathd` daemon is restarted, such as on a system restart.

15.6.1   Creating the /etc/multipath.conf File

1. Open a terminal console.

2. Copy one of the template files located in `/usr/share/doc/packages/multipath-tools/` to `/etc/multipath.conf`. Three different versions are available:

`multipath.conf.synthetic`

> Skeleton file that contains the general structure and example values.

`multipath.conf.annotated`

> Skeleton file that contains the general structure and example values and detailed comments.

`multipath.conf.defaults`

> This file contains the complete default settings, including the settings for all devices that are automatically detected. Using this file as a template is not recommended.

3. Ensure that there is an appropriate **device** entry for your SAN. Most vendors provide documentation on the proper setup of the **device** section.

   The `/etc/multipath.conf` file requires a different **device** section for different SANs. If you are using a storage subsystem that is automatically detected (see *Section 15.2.1, "Storage Arrays That Are Automatically Detected for Multipathing"*), the default entry for that device can be used; no further configuration of the `/etc/multipath.conf` file is required.

4. Save the file.

15.6.2   Sections in the `/etc/multipath.conf` File

The `/etc/multipath.conf` file is organized into the following sections. See `/usr/share/doc/packages/multipath-tools/multipath.conf.annotated` for a template with extensive comments for each of the attributes and their options.

defaults

> General default settings for multipath I/O. These values are used if no values are given in the appropriate device or multipath sections. For information, see *Section 15.7, "Configuring Default Policies for Polling, Queuing, and Failback"*.

blacklist

> Lists the device names to discard as not multipath candidates. Devices can be identified by their device node name (`devnode`), their WWID (`wwid`), or their vendor or product strings (`device`). You typically ignore non-multipathed devices, such as hpsa, fd, hd, md, dm, sr, scd, st, ram, raw, loop. For more information and examples, see *Section 15.8, "Blacklisting Non-Multipath Devices"*.

blacklist_exceptions

Lists the device names of devices to be treated as multipath candidates even if they are on the blacklist. Devices can be identified by their device node name (`devnode`), their WWID (`wwid`), or their vendor or product strings (`device`). You must specify the excepted devices by using the same keyword that you used in the blacklist. For example, if you used the devnode keyword for devices in the blacklist, you use the devnode keyword to exclude some devices in the blacklist exceptions. It is not possible to blacklist devices by using the `devnode` keyword and to exclude some of them by using the `wwid` keyword. For more information and examples, see *Section 15.8, "Blacklisting Non-Multipath Devices"*.

multipaths

Specifies settings for individual multipath devices. Except for settings that do not support individual settings, these values overwrite what is specified in the `defaults` and `devices` sections of the configuration file.

devices

Specifies settings for individual storage controllers. These values overwrite values specified in the `defaults` section of the configuration file. If you use a storage array that is not supported by default, you can create a `devices` subsection to specify the default settings for it. These values can be overwritten by settings for individual multipath devices if the keyword allows it.

For information, see the following:

- *Section 15.9, "Configuring User-Friendly Names or Alias Names"*

- *Section 15.14.6, "Configuring Default Settings for IBM z Systems Devices"*

15.6.3   Verifying the Multipath Setup in the /etc/multipath.conf File

Whenever you create or modify the `/etc/multipath.conf` file, the changes are not automatically applied when you save the file. You can perform a "dry run" of the setup to verify the multipath setup before you update the multipath maps.

At the server command prompt, enter

```
sudo multipath -v2 -d
```

This command scans the devices, then displays what the setup would look like if you commit the changes. It is assumed that the `multipathd` daemon is already running with the old (or default) multipath settings when you modify the `/etc/multipath.conf` file and perform the dry run. If the changes are acceptable, continue with the next step.

The output is similar to the following:

```
26353900f02796769
[size=127 GB]
[features="0"]
[hwhandler="1    emc"]

\_ round-robin 0 [first]
   \_ 1:0:1:2 sdav 66:240  [ready ]
   \_ 0:0:1:2 sdr  65:16   [ready ]

\_ round-robin 0
   \_ 1:0:0:2 sdag 66:0    [ready ]
   \_ 0:0:0:2 sdc  8:32    [ready ]
```

Paths are grouped into priority groups. Only one priority group is in active use at a time. To model an active/active configuration, all paths end in the same group. To model an active/passive configuration, the paths that should not be active in parallel are placed in several distinct priority groups. This normally happens automatically on device discovery.

The output shows the order, the scheduling policy used to balance I/O within the group, and the paths for each priority group. For each path, its physical address (host:bus:target:lun), device node name, major:minor number, and state is shown.

By using a verbosity level of -v3 in the dry run, you can see all detected paths, multipaths, and device maps. Both WWID and device node blacklisted devices are displayed.

The following is an example of -v3 output on a 64-bit SLES 11 SP2 server with two Qlogic HBAs connected to a Xiotech Magnitude 3000 SAN. Some multiple entries have been omitted to shorten the example.

```
tux > sudo multipath -v3 d
dm-22: device node name blacklisted
< content omitted >
loop7: device node name blacklisted
```

```
< content omitted >
md0: device node name blacklisted
< content omitted >
dm-0: device node name blacklisted
sdf: not found in pathvec
sdf: mask = 0x1f
sdf: dev_t = 8:80
sdf: size = 105005056
sdf: subsystem = scsi
sdf: vendor = XIOtech
sdf: product = Magnitude 3D
sdf: rev = 3.00
sdf: h:b:t:l = 1:0:0:2
sdf: tgt_node_name = 0x202100d0b2028da
sdf: serial = 000028DA0014
sdf: getuid= "/lib/udev/scsi_id --whitelisted --device=/dev/%n" (config file
 default)
sdf: uid = 200d0b2da28001400 (callout)
sdf: prio = const (config file default)
sdf: const prio = 1
[...]
ram15: device node name blacklisted
[...]
===== paths list =====
uuid                hcil      dev dev_t pri dm_st  chk_st  vend/prod/rev
200d0b2da28001400 1:0:0:2 sdf 8:80  1   [undef][undef] XIOtech,Magnitude 3D
200d0b2da28005400 1:0:0:1 sde 8:64  1   [undef][undef] XIOtech,Magnitude 3D
200d0b2da28004d00 1:0:0:0 sdd 8:48  1   [undef][undef] XIOtech,Magnitude 3D
200d0b2da28001400 0:0:0:2 sdc 8:32  1   [undef][undef] XIOtech,Magnitude 3D
200d0b2da28005400 0:0:0:1 sdb 8:16  1   [undef][undef] XIOtech,Magnitude 3D
200d0b2da28004d00 0:0:0:0 sda 8:0   1   [undef][undef] XIOtech,Magnitude 3D
params = 0 0 2 1 round-robin 0 1 1 8:80 1000 round-robin 0 1 1 8:32 1000
status = 2 0 0 0 2 1 A 0 1 0 8:80 A 0 E 0 1 0 8:32 A 0
sdf: mask = 0x4
sdf: path checker = directio (config file default)
directio: starting new request
```

```
directio: async io getevents returns 1 (errno=Success)
directio: io finished 4096/0
sdf: state = 2
[...]
```

15.6.4   Applying the /etc/multipath.conf File Changes to Update the Multipath Maps

Changes to the `/etc/multipath.conf` file cannot take effect when **multipathd** is running. After you make changes, save and close the file, then do the following to apply the changes and update the multipath maps:

1. Stop the `multipathd` service:

   ```
   sudo systemctl stop multipathd
   ```

2. Clear old multipath bindings by entering

   ```
   sudo /sbin/multipath -F
   ```

3. Create new multipath bindings by entering

   ```
   sudo /sbin/multipath -v2 -l
   ```

4. Restart the `multipathd` service:

   ```
   sudo systemctl start multipathd
   ```

5. Run **dracut -f** to re-create the `initrd` image on your system, then reboot in order for the changes to take effect.

15.7 Configuring Default Policies for Polling, Queuing, and Failback

The goal of multipath I/O is to provide connectivity fault tolerance between the storage system and the server. The desired default behavior depends on whether the server is a stand-alone server or a node in a high-availability cluster.

When you configure multipath I/O for a stand-alone server, the no_path_retry setting protects the server operating system from receiving I/O errors as long as possible. It queues messages until a multipath failover occurs and provides a healthy connection.

When you configure multipath I/O for a node in a high-availability cluster, you want multipath to report the I/O failure to trigger the resource failover instead of waiting for a multipath failover to be resolved. In cluster environments, you must modify the no_path_retry setting so that the cluster node receives an I/O error in relation to the cluster verification process (recommended to be 50% of the heartbeat tolerance) if the connection is lost to the storage system. In addition, you want the multipath I/O fallback to be set to manual to avoid a ping-pong of resources because of path failures.

The /etc/multipath.conf file should contain a **defaults** section where you can specify default behaviors for polling, queuing, and failback. If the field is not otherwise specified in a **device** section, the default setting is applied for that SAN configuration.

The following are the compiled default settings. They will be used unless you overwrite these values by creating and configuring a personalized /etc/multipath.conf file.

```
defaults {
  verbosity 2
#  udev_dir is deprecated in SLES 11 SP3
#  udev_dir               /dev
  polling_interval       5
#  path_selector default value is service-time in SLES 11 SP3
#  path_selector          "round-robin 0"
  path selector          "service-time 0"
  path_grouping_policy  failover
#  getuid_callout is deprecated in SLES 11 SP3 and replaced with uid_attribute
#  getuid_callout         "/lib/udev/scsi_id --whitelisted --device=/dev/%n"
#  uid_attribute is new in SLES 11 SP3
  uid_attribute          "ID_SERIAL"
```

```
    prio                        "const"
    prio_args                   ""
    features                    "0"
    path_checker                "directio"
    alias_prefix                "mpath"
    rr_min_io_rq                1
    max_fds                     "max"
    rr_weight                   "uniform"
    queue_without_daemon        "yes"
    flush_on_last_del           "no"
    user_friendly_names         "no"
    fast_io_fail_tmo            5
    bindings_file               "/etc/multipath/bindings"
    wwids_file                  "/etc/multipath/wwids"
    log_checker_err             "always"


    retain_attached_hw_handler  "no"
    detect_prio                 "no"
    failback                    "manual"
    no_path_retry               "fail"
    }
```

For information about setting the polling, queuing, and failback policies, see the following parameters in *Section 15.10, "Configuring Path Failover Policies and Priorities"*:

- *polling_interval*

- *no_path_retry*

- *failback*

If you modify the settings in the defaults section, the changes are not applied until you update the multipath maps, or until the multipathd daemon is restarted, such as at system restart.

15.8 Blacklisting Non-Multipath Devices

The `/etc/multipath.conf` file should contain a **blacklist** section where all non-multipath devices are listed. You can blacklist devices by WWID (`wwid` keyword), device name (`devnode` keyword), or device type (`device` section). You can also use the `blacklist_exceptions` section to enable multipath for some devices that are blacklisted by the regular expressions used in the `blacklist` section.

You typically ignore non-multipathed devices, such as hpsa, fd, hd, md, dm, sr, scd, st, ram, raw, and loop. For example, local IDE hard disks and flash disks do not normally have multiple paths. If you want **multipath** to ignore single-path devices, put them in the **blacklist** section.

 Note: Compatibility

The keyword `devnode_blacklist` has been deprecated and replaced with the keyword `blacklist`.

With SUSE Linux Enterprise Server 12 the glibc-provided regular expressions are used. To match an arbitrary string, you must now use `".*"` rather than just `"*"`.

For example, to blacklist local devices and all arrays from the `hpsa` driver from being managed by multipath, the **blacklist** section looks like this:

```
blacklist {
      wwid "26353900f02796769"
      devnode "^(ram|raw|loop|fd|md|dm-|sr|scd|st)[0-9]*"
      devnode "^sd[a-z][0-9]*"
}
```

You can also blacklist only the partitions from a driver instead of the entire array. For example, you can use the following regular expression to blacklist only partitions from the cciss driver and not the entire array:

```
blacklist {
      devnode "^cciss!c[0-9]d[0-9]*[p[0-9]*]"
}
```

You can blacklist by specific device types by adding a `device` section in the blacklist, and using the `vendor` and `product` keywords.

```
blacklist {
    device {
        vendor   "DELL"
        product ".*"
    }
}
```

You can use a `blacklist_exceptions` section to enable multipath for some devices that were blacklisted by the regular expressions used in the `blacklist` section. You add exceptions by WWID (`wwid` keyword), device name (`devnode` keyword), or device type (`device` section). You must specify the exceptions in the same way that you blacklisted the corresponding devices. That is, `wwid` exceptions apply to a `wwid` blacklist, `devnode` exceptions apply to a `devnode` blacklist, and device type exceptions apply to a device type blacklist.

For example, you can enable multipath for a desired device type when you have different device types from the same vendor. Blacklist all of the vendor's device types in the `blacklist` section, and then enable multipath for the desired device type by adding a `device` section in a `blacklist_exceptions` section.

```
blacklist {
    devnode "^(ram|raw|loop|fd|md|dm-|sr|scd|st|sda)[0-9]*"
    device {
        vendor   "DELL"
        product ".*"
    }
}

blacklist_exceptions {
    device {
        vendor   "DELL"
        product "MD3220i"
    }
}
```

You can also use the blacklist_exceptions to enable multipath only for specific devices. For example:

```
blacklist {
    wwid ".*"
}

blacklist_exceptions {
    wwid "3600d0230000000000e13955cc3751234"
    wwid "3600d0230000000000e13955cc3751235"
}
```

After you modify the `/etc/multipath.conf` file, you must run **dracut** `-f` to re-create the `initrd` on your system, then restart the server in order for the changes to take effect.

After you do this, the local devices should no longer be listed in the multipath maps when you issue the **multipath -ll** command.

15.9 Configuring User-Friendly Names or Alias Names

A multipath device can be identified by its WWID, by a user-friendly name, or by an alias that you assign for it. Device node names in the form of `/dev/sdn` and `/dev/dm-n` can change on reboot and might be assigned to different devices each time. A device's WWID, user-friendly name, and alias name persist across reboots, and are the preferred way to identify the device.

> ⓘ **Important: Using Persistent Names is Recommended**
>
> Because device node names in the form of `/dev/sdn` and `/dev/dm-n` can change on reboot, referring to multipath devices by their WWID is preferred. You can also use a user-friendly name or alias that is mapped to the WWID to identify the device uniquely across reboots.

The following table describes the types of device names that can be used for a device in the `/etc/multipath.conf` file. For an example of `multipath.conf` settings, see the `/usr/share/doc/packages/multipath-tools/multipath.conf.synthetic` file.

Name Types	Description
WWID (default)	The serial WWID (Worldwide Identifier) is an identifier for the multipath device that is guaranteed to be globally unique and unchanging. The default name used in multipathing is the ID of the logical unit as found in the `/dev/disk/by-id` directory. For example, a device with the WWID of `3600508e0000000009e6baa6f609e7908` is listed as `/dev/disk/by-id/scsi-3600508e0000000009e6baa6f609e7908`.
User-friendly	The Device Mapper Multipath device names in the `/dev/mapper` directory also reference the ID of the logical unit. These multipath device names are user-friendly names in the form of `/dev/mapper/mpathN`, such as `/dev/mapper/mpath0`. The names are unique and persistent because they use the `/var/lib/multipath/bindings` file to track the association between the UUID and user-friendly names.
Alias	An alias name is a globally unique name that the administrator provides for a multipath device. Alias names override the WWID and the user-friendly `/dev/mapper/mpathN` names. If you are using user_friendly_names, do not set the alias to mpath N format. This may conflict with an automatically assigned user-friendly name, and give you incorrect device node names.

The global multipath `user_friendly_names` option in the `/etc/multipath.conf` file is used to enable or disable the use of user-friendly names for multipath devices. If it is set to `no` (the default), multipath uses the WWID as the name of the device. If it is set to `yes`, multipath uses the `/var/lib/multipath/bindings` file to assign a persistent and unique name to the device in the form of mpath<n> in the `/dev/mapper` directory. The `bindings file` option in the `/etc/multipath.conf` file can be used to specify an alternate location for the `bindings` file.

The global multipath `alias` option in the `/etc/multipath.conf` file is used to explicitly assign a name to the device. If an alias name is set up for a multipath device, the alias is used instead of the WWID or the user-friendly name.

Using the `user_friendly_names` option can be problematic in the following situations:

Root Device Is Using Multipath:

If the system root device is using multipath and you use the `user_friendly_names` option, the user-friendly settings in the `/var/lib/multipath/bindings` file are included in the `initrd`. If you later change the storage setup, such as by adding or removing devices, there is a mismatch between the bindings setting inside the `initrd` and the bindings settings in `/var/lib/multipath/bindings`.

 Warning: Binding Mismatches

A bindings mismatch between `initrd` and `/var/lib/multipath/bindings` can lead to a wrong assignment of mount points to devices, which can result in file system corruption and data loss.

To avoid this problem, we recommend that you use the default WWID settings for the system root device. You should not use aliases for the system root device. Because the device name would differ, using an alias causes you to lose the ability to seamlessly switch off multipathing via the kernel command line.

Mounting /var from Another Partition:

The default location of the `user_friendly_names` configuration file is `/var/lib/multipath/bindings`. If the `/var` data is not located on the system root device but mounted from another partition, the `bindings` file is not available when setting up multipathing. Ensure that the `/var/lib/multipath/bindings` file is available on the system root device and multipath can find it. For example, this can be done as follows:

1. Move the `/var/lib/multipath/bindings` file to `/etc/multipath/bindings`.

2. Set the `bindings_file` option in the `defaults` section of `/etc/multipath.conf` to this new location. For example:

```
defaults {
          user_friendly_names yes
          bindings_file "/etc/multipath/bindings"
}
```

Configuring User-Friendly Names or Alias Names

Multipath Is in the initrd:

Even if the system root device is not on multipath, it is possible for multipath to be included in the `initrd`. For example, this can happen if the system root device is on LVM. If you use the `user_friendly_names` option and multipath is in the `initrd`, you should boot with the parameter **multipath=off** to avoid problems.

This disables multipath only in the `initrd` during system boots. After the system boots, the `boot.multipath` and `multipathd` boot scripts can activate multipathing.

Multipathing in HA Clusters:

See *Section 15.9.1, "Multipath Device Names in HA Clusters"* for details.

To enable user-friendly names or to specify aliases:

1. Open the `/etc/multipath.conf` file in a text editor with `root` privileges.

2. (Optional) Modify the location of the `/var/lib/multipath/bindings` file.
   The alternate path must be available on the system root device where multipath can find it.

   a. Move the `/var/lib/multipath/bindings` file to `/etc/multipath/bindings`.

   b. Set the `bindings_file` option in the `defaults` section of `/etc/multipath.conf` to this new location. For example:

   ```
   defaults {
           user_friendly_names yes
           bindings_file "/etc/multipath/bindings"
   }
   ```

3. (Optional, not recommended) Enable user-friendly names:

   a. Uncomment the `defaults` section and its ending bracket.

   b. Uncomment the `user_friendly_names option`, then change its value from No to Yes.
      For example:

   ```
   ## Use user-friendly names, instead of using WWIDs as names.
   defaults {
   ```

Configuring User-Friendly Names or Alias Names

```
      user_friendly_names yes
}
```

4. (Optional) Specify your own names for devices by using the **alias** option in the **multipath** section.

For example:

```
## Use alias names, instead of using WWIDs as names.
multipaths {
        multipath {
                wwid            3600604800002835013125359 4d303030
                alias             blue1
        }
        multipath {
                wwid            3600604800002835013125359 4d303041
                alias             blue2
        }
        multipath {
                wwid            3600604800002835013125359 4d303145
                alias             yellow1
        }
        multipath {
                wwid            3600604800002835013125359 4d303334
                alias             yellow2
        }
}
```

! Important: WWWID vs. WWN

When you define device aliases in the `/etc/multipath.conf` file, ensure that you use each device's WWID (such as `3600508e0000000009e6baa6f609e7908`) and not its WWN, which replaces the first character of a device ID with `0x`, such as `0x600508e0000000009e6baa6f609e7908`.

5. Save your changes, then close the file.

The changes are not applied until you update the multipath maps, or until the `multipathd` daemon is restarted.

If you want to use the entire LUN directly (for example, if you are using the SAN features to partition your storage), you can use the `/dev/disk/by-id/xxx` names for `mkfs`, `fstab`, your application, and so on. Partitioned devices have `_part<n>` appended to the device name, such as `/dev/disk/by-id/xxx_part1`.

In the `/dev/disk/by-id` directory, the multipath-mapped devices are represented by the device's `dm-uuid*` name or alias name (if you assign an alias for it in the `/etc/multipath.conf` file). The `scsi-` and `wwn-` device names represent physical paths to the devices.

15.9.1　Multipath Device Names in HA Clusters

Ensure that multipath devices have the same name across all devices by doing the following:

- Use UUID and alias names to ensure that multipath device names are consistent across all nodes in the cluster. Alias names must be unique across all nodes. Copy the `/etc/multipath.conf` file from the node to the `/etc/` directory for all of the other nodes in the cluster.

- When using links to multipath-mapped devices, ensure that you specify the `dm-uuid*` name or alias name in the `/dev/disk/by-id` directory, and not a fixed path instance of the device. For information, see *Section 15.9, "Configuring User-Friendly Names or Alias Names"*.

- Set the `user_friendly_names` configuration option to `no` to disable it. A user-friendly name is unique to a node, but a device might not be assigned the same user-friendly name on every node in the cluster.

  If you really need to use user-friendly names, you can force the system-defined user-friendly names to be consistent across all nodes in the cluster by doing the following:

  1. In the `/etc/multipath.conf` file on one node:

     a. Set the `user_friendly_names` configuration option to `yes` to enable it. Multipath uses the `/var/lib/multipath/bindings` file to assign a persistent and unique name to the device in the form of `mpath<n>` in the `/dev/mapper` directory.

     b. (Optional) Set the `bindings_file` option in the `defaults` section of the `/etc/multipath.conf` file to specify an alternate location for the `bindings` file.

The default location is `/var/lib/multipath/bindings`.

2. Set up all of the multipath devices on the node.

3. Copy the `/etc/multipath.conf` file from the node to the `/etc/` directory of all the other nodes in the cluster.

4. Copy the `bindings` file from the node to the `bindings_file` path on all of the other nodes in the cluster.

15.10   Configuring Path Failover Policies and Priorities

In a Linux host, when there are multiple paths to a storage controller, each path appears as a separate block device, and results in multiple block devices for single LUN. The Device Mapper Multipath service detects multiple paths with the same LUN ID, and creates a new multipath device with that ID. For example, a host with two HBAs attached to a storage controller with two ports via a single unzoned Fibre Channel switch sees four block devices: `/dev/sda`, `/dev/sdb`, `/dev/sdc`, and `/dev/sdd`. The Device Mapper Multipath service creates a single block device, `/dev/mpath/mpath1`, that reroutes I/O through those four underlying block devices.

This section describes how to specify policies for failover and configure priorities for the paths. Note that changes to `/etc/multipath.conf` are not applied until you update the multipath maps, or until the `multipathd` daemon is restarted.

15.10.1   Configuring the Path Failover Policies

Use the **multipath** command with the `-p` option to set the path failover policy:

```
sudo multipath devicename -p policy
```

Replace *policy* with one of the following policy options:

TABLE 15.5: GROUP POLICY OPTIONS FOR THE MULTIPATH -P COMMAND

Policy Option	Description
failover	(Default) One path per priority group.

Policy Option	Description
multibus	All paths in one priority group.
group_by_serial	One priority group per detected serial number.
group_by_prio	One priority group per path priority value. Priorities are determined by callout programs specified as a global, per-controller, or per-multipath option in the `/etc/multipath.conf` configuration file.
group_by_node_name	One priority group per target node name. Target node names are fetched in the `/sys/class/fc_transport/target*/node_name` location.

15.10.2   Configuring Failover Priorities

You must manually enter the failover priorities for the device in the `/etc/multipath.conf` file. Examples for all settings and options can be found in the `/usr/share/doc/packages/multipath-tools/multipath.conf.annotated` file.

15.10.2.1   Understanding Priority Groups and Attributes

A *priority group* is a collection of paths that go to the same physical LUN. By default, I/O is distributed in a round-robin fashion across all paths in the group. The **multipath** command automatically creates priority groups for each LUN in the SAN based on the `path_grouping_policy` setting for that SAN. The **multipath** command multiplies the number of paths in a group by the group's priority to determine which group is the primary. The group with the highest calculated value is the primary. When all paths in the primary group are failed, the priority group with the next highest value becomes active.

A *path priority* is an integer value assigned to a path. The higher the value, the higher the priority. An external program is used to assign priorities for each path. For a given device, the paths with the same priorities belong to the same priority group.

The `prio` setting is used in the `defaults{}` or `devices{}` section of the `/etc/multipath.conf` file. It is silently ignored when it is specified for an individual `multipath` definition in the `multipaths{}` section. The `prio` line specifies the prioritizer. If the prioritizer requires an argument, you specify the argument by using the `prio_args` keyword on a second line.

PRIO Settings for the Defaults or Devices Sections

prio

Specifies the prioritizer program to call to obtain a path priority value. Weights are summed for each path group to determine the next path group to use in case of failure.

Use the `prio_args` keyword to specify arguments if the specified prioritizer requires arguments.

If no `prio` keyword is specified, all paths are equal. The default setting is `const` with a `prio_args` setting with no value.

```
prio "const"
prio_args ""
```

Example prioritizer programs include:

Prioritizer Program	Description
alua	Generates path priorities based on the SCSI-3 ALUA settings.
const	Generates the same priority for all paths.
emc	Generates the path priority for EMC arrays.
hdc	Generates the path priority for Hitachi HDS Modular storage arrays.
hp_sw	Generates the path priority for Compaq/HP controller in active/standby mode.
ontap	Generates the path priority for NetApp arrays.
random	Generates a random priority for each path.

Configuring Failover Priorities

Prioritizer Program	Description
rdac	Generates the path priority for LSI/Engenio RDAC controller.

weightedpath	Generates the path priority based on the weighted values you specify in the arguments for `prio_args`, such as:
	
	`[hbtl|devname] regex1 prio1 regex2 prio2...`
	
	The `hbtl regex` argument format uses the SCSI `H:B:T:L` notation (such as `1:0:.:.` and `*:0:0:.`) with a weight value, where H, B, T, L are the host, bus, target, and LUN IDs for a device. For example:
	
	`prio "weightedpath"`
	`prio_args "hbtl 1:.:.:. 2 4:.:.:. 4"`
	
	The devname regular expression argument format uses a device node name with a weight value for each device. For example:
	
	`prio "weightedpath"`
	`prio_args "devname sda 50 sde 10 sdc 50 sdf 10"`

prio_args

> Specifies the arguments for the specified prioritizer program that requires arguments. Most `prio` programs do not need arguments.
>
> There is no default. The value depends on the `prio` setting and whether the prioritizer requires arguments.

Multipath Attributes

Multipath attributes are used to control the behavior of multipath I/O for devices. You can specify attributes as defaults for all multipath devices. You can also specify attributes that apply only to a given multipath device by creating an entry for that device in the `multipaths` section of the multipath configuration file.

Configuring Failover Priorities

user_friendly_names

Specifies whether to use world-wide IDs (WWIDs) or to use the `/var/lib/multi-path/bindings` file to assign a persistent and unique alias to the multipath devices in the form of `/dev/mapper/mpathN`.

This option can be used in the `devices` section and the `multipaths` section.

Value	Description
no	(Default) Use the WWIDs shown in the `/dev/disk/by-id/` location.
yes	Autogenerate user-friendly names as aliases for the multipath devices instead of the actual ID.

failback

Specifies whether to monitor the failed path recovery, and indicates the timing for group failback after failed paths return to service.

When the failed path recovers, the path is added back into the multipath-enabled path list based on this setting. Multipath evaluates the priority groups, and changes the active priority group when the priority of the primary path exceeds the secondary group.

Value	Description
manual	(Default) The failed path is not monitored for recovery. The administrator runs the **multipath** command to update enabled paths and priority groups.
immediate	When a path recovers, enable the path immediately.
n	When the path recovers, wait n seconds before enabling the path. Specify an integer value greater than 0.

We recommend failback setting of `manual` for multipath in cluster environments to prevent multipath failover ping-pong.

```
failback "manual"
```

Configuring Failover Priorities

Important: Verification

Ensure that you verify the failback setting with your storage system vendor. Different storage systems can require different settings.

no_path_retry

Specifies the behaviors to use on path failure.

Value	Description
n	Specifies the number of retries until **multipath** stops the queuing and fails the path. Specify an integer value greater than 0. In a cluster, you can specify a value of "0" to prevent queuing and allow resources to fail over.
fail	Specifies immediate failure (no queuing).
queue	Never stop queuing (queue forever until the path comes alive).

We recommend a retry setting of `fail` or `0` in the `/etc/multipath.conf` file when working in a cluster. This causes the resources to fail over when the connection is lost to storage. Otherwise, the messages queue and the resource failover cannot occur.

```
no_path_retry "fail"
no_path_retry "0"
```

 Important: Verification

Ensure that you verify the retry settings with your storage system vendor. Different storage systems can require different settings.

path_checker

Determines the state of the path.

Value	Description
directio	Reads the first sector that has direct I/O. This is useful for DASD devices. Logs failure messages in the `systemd` journal (see Book *"Administration Guide"*, *Chapter 10* **"journalctl**: *Query the* `systemd` *Journal"*).
tur	Issues an SCSI test unit ready command to the device. This is the preferred setting if the LUN supports it. On failure, the command does not fill up the `systemd` log journal with messages.
custom_vendor_value	Some SAN vendors provide custom path_checker options: • **cciss_tur:** Checks the path state for HP Smart Storage Arrays. • **emc_clariion:** Queries the EMC Clariion EVPD page 0xC0 to determine the path state. • **hp_sw:** Checks the path state (Up, Down, or Ghost) for HP storage arrays with Active/Standby firmware. • **rdac:** Checks the path state for the LSI/Engenio RDAC storage controller.

path_grouping_policy

Specifies the path grouping policy for a multipath device hosted by a given controller.

Value	Description
failover	(Default) One path is assigned per priority group so that only one path at a time is used.
multibus	All valid paths are in one priority group. Traffic is load-balanced across all active paths in the group.
group_by_prio	One priority group exists for each path priority value. Paths with the same priority are in the same priority group. Priorities are assigned by an external program.
group_by_serial	Paths are grouped by the SCSI target serial number (controller node WWN).
group_by_node_name	One priority group is assigned per target node name. Target node names are fetched in `/sys/class/fc_transport/target*/node_name`.

path_selector

Specifies the path-selector algorithm to use for load balancing.

Value	Description
round-robin 0	The load-balancing algorithm used to balance traffic across all active paths in a priority group.
queue-length 0	A dynamic load balancer that balances the number of in-flight I/O on paths similar to the least-pending option.
service-time 0	(Default) A service-time oriented load balancer that balances I/O on paths according to the latency.

pg_timeout

Specifies path group timeout handling. No value can be specified; an internal default is set.

polling_interval

Specifies the time in seconds between the end of one path checking cycle and the beginning of the next path checking cycle.

Specify an integer value greater than 0. The default value is 5. Ensure that you verify the polling_interval setting with your storage system vendor. Different storage systems can require different settings.

rr_min_io_rq

Specifies the number of I/O requests to route to a path before switching to the next path in the current path group, using request-based device-mapper-multipath.

Specify an integer value greater than 0. The default value is 1.

```
rr_min_io_rq "1"
```

rr_weight

Specifies the weighting method to use for paths.

Value	Description
uniform	(Default) All paths have the same round-robin weights.
priorities	Each path's weight is determined by the path's priority times the rr_min_io_rq setting.

uid_attribute

A udev attribute that provides a unique path identifier. The default value is ID_SERIAL.

15.10.2.2   Configuring for Round-Robin Load Balancing

All paths are active. I/O is configured for some number of seconds or some number of I/O transactions before moving to the next open path in the sequence.

15.10.2.3   Configuring for Single Path Failover

A single path with the highest priority (lowest value setting) is active for traffic. Other paths are available for failover, but are not used unless failover occurs.

15.10.2.4 Grouping I/O Paths for Round-Robin Load Balancing

Multiple paths with the same priority fall into the active group. When all paths in that group fail, the device fails over to the next highest priority group. All paths in the group share the traffic load in a round-robin load balancing fashion.

15.10.3 Reporting Target Path Groups

Use the SCSI Report Target Port Groups (`sg_rtpg(8)`) command. For information, see the man page for `sg_rtpg(8)`.

15.11 Configuring Multipath I/O for the Root Device

Device Mapper Multipath I/O (DM-MPIO) is available and supported for `/boot` and `/root` in SUSE Linux Enterprise Server. In addition, the YaST partitioner in the YaST installer supports enabling multipath during the install.

15.11.1 Enabling Multipath I/O at Install Time

The multipath software must be running at install time if you want to install the operating system on a multipath device. The `multipathd` daemon is not automatically active during the system installation. You can start it by using the *Configure Multipath* option in the YaST Partitioner.

15.11.1.1 Enabling Multipath I/O at Install Time on an Active/Active Multipath Storage LUN

1. Choose *Expert Partitioner* on the *Suggested Partitioning* screen during the installation.

2. Select the *Hard Disks* main icon, click the *Configure* button, then select *Configure Multipath*.

3. Start multipath.
   YaST starts to rescan the disks and shows available multipath devices (such as `/dev/disk/by-id/dm-uuid-mpath-3600a0b80000f4593000012ae4ab0ae65`). This is the device that should be used for all further processing.

4. Click *Next* to continue with the installation.

15.11.1.2   Enabling Multipath I/O at Install Time on an Active/Passive Multipath Storage LUN

The `multipathd` daemon is not automatically active during the system installation. You can start it by using the *Configure Multipath* option in the YaST Partitioner.

To enable multipath I/O at install time for an active/passive multipath storage LUN:

1. Choose *Expert Partitioner* on the *Suggested Partitioning* screen during the installation.

2. Select the *Hard Disks* main icon, click the *Configure* button, then select *Configure Multipath*.

3. Start multipath.
   YaST starts to rescan the disks and shows available multipath devices (such as `/dev/disk/by-id/dm-uuid-mpath-3600a0b80000f4593000012ae4ab0ae65`). This is the device that should be used for all further processing. Write down the device path and UUID; you will need it later.

4. Click *Next* to continue with the installation.

5. After all settings are done and the installation is finished, YaST starts to write the boot loader information, and displays a countdown to restart the system. Stop the counter by clicking the *Stop* button and press `Ctrl`‑`Alt`‑`F5` to access a console.

6. Use the console to determine if a passive path was entered in the `/boot/grub2/device.map` file for the `hd0` entry.
   This is necessary because the installation does not distinguish between active and passive paths.

   a. Mount the root device to `/mnt` by entering

   ```
   mount /dev/disk/by-id/UUID;_part2 /mnt
   ```

   For example, enter

   ```
   mount /dev/disk/by-id/dm-uuid-
   mpath-3600a0b80000f4593000012ae4ab0ae65_part2 /mnt
   ```

b. Mount the boot device to `/mnt/boot` by entering

```
mount /dev/disk/by-id/UUID_part1 /mnt/boot
```

For example, enter

```
mount /dev/disk/by-id/dm-uuid-
mpath-3600a0b80000f4593000012ae4ab0ae65_part2 /mnt/boot
```

c. In the `/mnt/boot/grub2/device.map` file, determine if the `hd0` entry points to a passive path, then do one of the following:

- **Active path:** No action is needed. Skip all remaining steps and return to the YaST graphical environment by pressing Ctrl Alt F7 and continue with the installation.

- **Passive path:** The configuration must be changed and the boot loader must be reinstalled.

7. If the `hd0` entry points to a passive path, change the configuration and reinstall the boot loader:

a. Enter the following commands at the console prompt:

```
mount -o bind /dev /mnt/dev
mount -o bind /sys /mnt/sys
mount -o bind /proc /mnt/proc
chroot /mnt
```

b. At the console, run **multipath -ll**, then check the output to find the active path. Passive paths are flagged as `ghost`.

c. In the `/boot/grub2/device.map` file, change the `hd0` entry to an active path, save the changes, and close the file.

d. Reinstall the boot loader by entering

```
grub-install /dev/disk/by-id/UUID_part1 /mnt/boot
```

For example, enter

```
grub-install /dev/disk/by-id/dm-uuid-
mpath-3600a0b80000f4593000012ae4ab0ae65_part2 /mnt/boot
```

e. Enter the following commands:

```
exit
umount /mnt/*
umount /mnt
```

8. Return to the YaST graphical environment by pressing Ctrl – Alt – F7.

9. Click *OK* to continue with the installation reboot.

15.11.2 Enabling Multipath I/O for an Existing Root Device

1. Install Linux with only a single path active, preferably one where the `by-id` symbolic links are listed in the partitioner.

2. Mount the devices by using the `/dev/disk/by-id` path used during the install.

3. Add dm-multipath to `/etc/dracut.conf.d/01-dist.conf` by adding the following line:

```
force_drivers+="dm-multipath"
```

4. For System Z, before running **dracut**, edit the `/etc/zipl.conf` file to change the by-path information in `zipl.conf` with the same by-id information that was used in `/etc/fstab`.

5. Run **dracut** `-f` to update the `initrd` image.

6. For System Z, after running **dracut**, run **zipl**.

7. Reboot the server.

15.11.3   Disabling Multipath I/O on the Root Device

- Add `multipath=off` to the kernel command line. This can be done with the YaST Boot Loader module. Open *Boot Loader Installation* › *Kernel Parameters* and add the parameter to both command lines.

  This affects only the root device. All other devices are not affected.

15.12   Using LVM2 on Multipath Devices

Ensure that the configuration file for `lvm.conf` points to the multipath-device names instead of fixed path names. This should happen automatically if `boot.multipath` is enabled and loads before `boot.lvm`.

15.12.1   Adding a Multipath Device Filter in the /etc/lvm/lvm.conf File

By default, LVM2 does not recognize multipathed devices. To make LVM2 recognize the multipathed devices as possible physical volumes, you must modify `/etc/lvm/lvm.conf` to scan multipathed devices through the multipath I/O layer.

Adding a multipath filter prevents LVM from scanning and using the physical paths for raw device nodes that represent individual paths to the SAN (/dev/sd*). Ensure that you specify the filter path so that LVM scans only the device mapper names for the device (`/dev/disk/by-id/dm-uuid-.*-mpath-.*`) after multipathing is configured.

To modify `/etc/lvm/lvm.conf` for multipath use:

1. Open the `/etc/lvm/lvm.conf` file in a text editor.

   If `/etc/lvm/lvm.conf` does not exist, you can create one based on your current LVM configuration by entering the following at a terminal console prompt:

   ```
   sudo lvm dumpconfig > /etc/lvm/lvm.conf
   ```

2. Change the `filter` and `types` entries in `/etc/lvm/lvm.conf` as follows:

   ```
   filter = [ "a|/dev/disk/by-id/.*|", "r|.*|" ]
   ```

```
types = [ "device-mapper", 1 ]
```

This allows LVM2 to scan only the by-id paths and reject everything else.

If you are using user-friendly names, specify the filter path so that only the Device Mapper names are scanned after multipathing is configured. The following filter path accepts only partitions on a multipathed device:

```
filter = [ "a|/dev/disk/by-id/dm-uuid-.*-mpath-.*|", "r|.*|" ]
```

To accept both raw disks and partitions for Device Mapper names, specify the path as follows, with no hyphen (-) before `mpath`:

```
filter = [ "a|/dev/disk/by-id/dm-uuid-.*mpath-.*|", "r|.*|" ]
```

3. If you are also using LVM2 on non-multipathed devices, make the necessary adjustments in the `filter` and `types` entries to suit your setup. Otherwise, the other LVM devices are not visible with a **pvscan** after you modify the `lvm.conf` file for multipathing.

   You want only those devices that are configured with LVM to be included in the LVM cache, so ensure that you are specific about which other non-multipathed devices are included by the filter.

   For example, if your local disk is `/dev/sda` and all SAN devices are `/dev/sdb` and above, specify the local and multipathing paths in the filter as follows:

```
filter = [ "a|/dev/sda.*|", "a|/dev/disk/by-id/.*|", "r|.*|" ]
types = [ "device-mapper", 253 ]
```

4. Save the file.

5. Add dm-multipath to `/etc/dracut.conf.d/01-dist.conf` by adding the following line:

```
force_drivers+="dm-multipath"
```

6. Make a new `initrd` to ensure that the Device Mapper Multipath services are loaded with the changed settings. Running **dracut** is needed only if the root (/) device or any parts of it (such as `/var`, `/etc`, `/log`) are on the SAN and multipath is needed to boot. Enter the following at a terminal console prompt:

```
dracut -f --add-drivers multipath
```

7. Reboot the server to apply the changes.

15.13 Configuring Multipath I/O for an Existing Software RAID

Ideally, you should configure multipathing for devices before you use them as components of a software RAID device. If you add multipathing after creating any software RAID devices, the DM-MPIO service might be starting after the `multipath` service on reboot, which makes multipathing appear not to be available for RAIDs. You can use the procedure in this section to get multipathing running for a previously existing software RAID.

For example, you might need to configure multipathing for devices in a software RAID under the following circumstances:

- If you create a new software RAID as part of the Partitioning settings during a new install or upgrade.

- If you did not configure the devices for multipathing before using them in the software RAID as a member device or spare.

- If you grow your system by adding new HBA adapters to the server or expanding the storage subsystem in your SAN.

 Note: Assumptions

The following instructions assume the software RAID device is `/dev/mapper/mpath0`, which is its device name as recognized by the kernel. It assumes you have enabled user-friendly names in the `/etc/multipath.conf` file as described in *Section 15.9, "Configuring User-Friendly Names or Alias Names"*.

Ensure that you modify the instructions for the device name of your software RAID.

1. Open a terminal console.
   Except where otherwise directed, use this console to enter the commands in the following steps.

2. If any software RAID devices are currently mounted or running, enter the following commands for each device to unmount the device and stop it.

```
sudo umount /dev/mapper/mpath0
sudo mdadm --misc --stop /dev/mapper/mpath0
```

3. Stop the **md** service by entering

```
sudo systemctl stop mdmonitor
```

4. Start the `multipathd` daemon by entering the following command:

```
systemctl start multipathd
```

5. After the multipathing service has been started, verify that the software RAID's component devices are listed in the `/dev/disk/by-id` directory. Do one of the following:

   - **Devices Are Listed:** The device names should now have symbolic links to their Device Mapper Multipath device names, such as `/dev/dm-1`.

   - **Devices Are Not Listed:** Force the multipath service to recognize them by flushing and rediscovering the devices by entering

   ```
   sudo multipath -F
   sudo multipath -v0
   ```

   The devices should now be listed in `/dev/disk/by-id`, and have symbolic links to their Device Mapper Multipath device names. For example:

   ```
   lrwxrwxrwx 1 root root 10 2011-01-06 11:42 dm-uuid-
   mpath-36006016088d014007e0d0d2213ecdf11 -> ../../dm-1
   ```

6. Restart the `mdmonitor` service and the RAID device by entering

```
systemctl start mdmonitor
```

7. Check the status of the software RAID by entering

```
mdadm --detail /dev/mapper/mpath0
```

The RAID's component devices should match their Device Mapper Multipath device names that are listed as the symbolic links of devices in the `/dev/disk/by-id` directory.

8. Make a new `initrd` to ensure that the Device Mapper Multipath services are loaded before the RAID services on reboot. Running **dracut** is needed only if the root (/) device or any parts of it (such as `/var`, `/etc`, `/log`) are on the SAN and multipath is needed to boot.

   Enter

   ```
   dracut -f --add-drivers multipath
   ```

9. Reboot the server to apply these post-install configuration settings.

10. Verify that the software RAID array comes up properly on top of the multipathed devices by checking the RAID status. Enter

   ```
   mdadm --detail /dev/mapper/mpath0
   ```

   For example:

   ```
   Number Major Minor RaidDevice State
   0 253 0 0 active sync /dev/dm-0
   1 253 1 1 active sync /dev/dm-1
   2 253 2 2 active sync /dev/dm-2
   ```

 Note: Using mdadm with Multipath Devices

The **mdadm** tool requires that the devices be accessed by the ID rather than by the device node path. Refer to *Section 15.4.3, "Using MDADM for Multipathed Devices"* for details.

15.14 Best Practice

15.14.1 Scanning for New Devices without Rebooting

If your system has already been configured for multipathing and you later need to add more storage to the SAN, you can use the **rescan-scsi-bus.sh** script to scan for the new devices. By default, this script scans all HBAs with typical LUN ranges. The general syntax for the command looks like the following:

```
rescan-scsi-bus.sh [options] [host [host ...]]
```

For most storage subsystems, the script can be run successfully without options. However, some special cases might need to use one or more options. Run **rescan-scsi-bus.sh --help** for details.

 Warning: EMC PowerPath Environments

> In EMC PowerPath environments, do not use the `rescan-scsi-bus.sh` utility provided with the operating system or the HBA vendor scripts for scanning the SCSI buses. To avoid potential file system corruption, EMC requires that you follow the procedure provided in the vendor documentation for EMC PowerPath for Linux.

Use the following procedure to scan the devices and make them available to multipathing without rebooting the system.

1. On the storage subsystem, use the vendor's tools to allocate the device and update its access control settings to allow the Linux system access to the new storage. Refer to the vendor's documentation for details.

2. Scan all targets for a host to make its new device known to the middle layer of the Linux kernel's SCSI subsystem. At a terminal console prompt, enter

```
sudo rescan-scsi-bus.sh
```

Depending on your setup, you might need to run **rescan-scsi-bus.sh** with optional parameters. Refer to **rescan-scsi-bus.sh --help** for details.

3. Check for scanning progress in the `systemd` journal (see *Book "Administration Guide"*, *Chapter 10 "***journalctl***: Query the* systemd *Journal"* for details). At a terminal console prompt, enter

```
sudo journalctl -r
```

This command displays the last lines of the log. For example:

```
tux > sudo journalctl -r
Feb 14 01:03 kernel: SCSI device sde: 81920000
Feb 14 01:03 kernel: SCSI device sdf: 81920000
Feb 14 01:03 multipathd: sde: path checker registered
Feb 14 01:03 multipathd: sdf: path checker registered
Feb 14 01:03 multipathd: mpath4: event checker started
Feb 14 01:03 multipathd: mpath5: event checker started
Feb 14 01:03:multipathd: mpath4: remaining active paths: 1
Feb 14 01:03 multipathd: mpath5: remaining active paths: 1
[...]
```

4. Repeat the previous steps to add paths through other HBA adapters on the Linux system that are connected to the new device.

5. Run the **multipath** command to recognize the devices for DM-MPIO configuration. At a terminal console prompt, enter

```
sudo multipath
```

You can now configure the new device for multipathing.

15.14.2   Scanning for New Partitioned Devices without Rebooting

Use the example in this section to detect a newly added multipathed LUN without rebooting.

 Warning: EMC PowerPath Environments

In EMC PowerPath environments, do not use the `rescan-scsi-bus.sh` utility provided with the operating system or the HBA vendor scripts for scanning the SCSI buses. To avoid potential file system corruption, EMC requires that you follow the procedure provided in the vendor documentation for EMC PowerPath for Linux.

1. Open a terminal console.

2. Scan all targets for a host to make its new device known to the middle layer of the Linux kernel's SCSI subsystem. At a terminal console prompt, enter

```
rescan-scsi-bus.sh
```

Depending on your setup, you might need to run **rescan-scsi-bus.sh** with optional parameters. Refer to **rescan-scsi-bus.sh --help** for details.

3. Verify that the device is seen (such as if the link has a new time stamp) by entering

```
ls -lrt /dev/dm-*
```

You can also verify the devices in /dev/disk/by-id by entering

```
ls -l /dev/disk/by-id/
```

4. Verify the new device appears in the log by entering

```
sudo journalctl -r
```

5. Use a text editor to add a new alias definition for the device in the /etc/multipath.conf file, such as data_vol3.
For example, if the UUID is 36006016088d014006e98a7a94a85db11, make the following changes:

```
defaults {
     user_friendly_names    yes
  }
multipaths {
     multipath {
          wwid     36006016088d014006e98a7a94a85db11
          alias    data_vol3
          }
  }
```

6. Create a partition table for the device by entering

```
fdisk /dev/disk/by-id/dm-uuid-mpath-<UUID>
```

Replace UUID with the device WWID, such as 36006016088d014006e98a7a94a85db11.

7. Trigger udev by entering

```
sudo echo 'add' > /sys/block/dm_device/uevent
```

For example, to generate the device-mapper devices for the partitions on dm-8, enter

```
sudo echo 'add' > /sys/block/dm-8/uevent
```

8. Create a file system on the device /dev/disk/by-id/dm-uuid-mpath-*UUID_partN*. Depending on your choice for the file system, you may use one of the following commands for this purpose: **mkfs.btrfs mkfs.ext3**, **mkfs.ext4**, or **mkfs.xfs**. Refer to the respective man pages for details. Replace UUID_partN with the actual UUID and partition number, such as 36006016088d014006e98a7a94a85db11_part1.

9. Create a label for the new partition by entering the following command:

```
sudo tune2fs -L LABELNAME /dev/disk/by-id/dm-uuid-UUID_partN
```

Replace UUID_partN with the actual UUID and partition number, such as 36006016088d014006e98a7a94a85db11_part1. Replace LABELNAME with a label of your choice.

10. Reconfigure DM-MPIO to let it read the aliases by entering

```
sudo multipathd -k'reconfigure'
```

11. Verify that the device is recognized by multipathd by entering

```
sudo multipath -ll
```

12. Use a text editor to add a mount entry in the /etc/fstab file.
At this point, the alias you created in a previous step is not yet in the /dev/disk/by-label directory. Add a mount entry for the /dev/dm-9 path, then change the entry before the next time you reboot to

```
LABEL=LABELNAME
```

13. Create a directory to use as the mount point, then mount the device.

15.14.3 Viewing Multipath I/O Status

Querying the multipath I/O status outputs the current status of the multipath maps.

The `multipath -l` option displays the current path status as of the last time that the path checker was run. It does not run the path checker.

The `multipath -ll` option runs the path checker, updates the path information, then displays the current status information. This option always displays the latest information about the path status.

• At a terminal console prompt, enter

```
sudo multipath -ll
```

This displays information for each multipathed device. For example:

```
tux > sudo multipath -ll
3600601607cf30e00184589a37a31d911
[size=127 GB][features="0"][hwhandler="1 emc"]

\_ round-robin 0 [active][first]
  \_ 1:0:1:2 sdav 66:240  [ready ][active]
  \_ 0:0:1:2 sdr  65:16   [ready ][active]

\_ round-robin 0 [enabled]
  \_ 1:0:0:2 sdag 66:0    [ready ][active]
  \_ 0:0:0:2 sdc  8:32    [ready ][active]
```

For each device, it shows the device's ID, size, features, and hardware handlers.

Paths to the device are automatically grouped into priority groups on device discovery. Only one priority group is active at a time. For an active/active configuration, all paths are in the same group. For an active/passive configuration, the passive paths are placed in separate priority groups.

The following information is displayed for each group:

- Scheduling policy used to balance I/O within the group, such as round-robin

- Whether the group is active, disabled, or enabled

- Whether the group is the first (highest priority) group

- Paths contained within the group

The following information is displayed for each path:

- The physical address as *host:bus:target:lun*, such as 1:0:1:2

- Device node name, such as sda

- Major:minor numbers

- Status of the device

15.14.4   Managing I/O in Error Situations

You might need to configure multipathing to queue I/O if all paths fail concurrently by enabling queue_if_no_path. Otherwise, I/O fails immediately if all paths are gone. In certain scenarios, where the driver, the HBA, or the fabric experience spurious errors, DM-MPIO should be configured to queue all I/O where those errors lead to a loss of all paths, and never propagate errors upward.

When you use multipathed devices in a cluster, you might choose to disable queue_if_no_path. This automatically fails the path instead of queuing the I/O, and escalates the I/O error to cause a failover of the cluster resources.

Because enabling queue_if_no_path leads to I/O being queued indefinitely unless a path is reinstated, ensure that **multipathd** is running and works for your scenario. Otherwise, I/O might be stalled indefinitely on the affected multipathed device until reboot or until you manually return to failover instead of queuing.

To test the scenario:

1. Open a terminal console.

2. Activate queuing instead of failover for the device I/O by entering

```
sudo dmsetup message device_ID 0 queue_if_no_path
```

Replace the *device_ID* with the ID for your device. The 0 value represents the sector and is used when sector information is not needed.
For example, enter:

```
sudo dmsetup message 3600601607cf30e00184589a37a31d911 0 queue_if_no_path
```

3. Return to failover for the device I/O by entering

```
sudo dmsetup message device_ID 0 fail_if_no_path
```

This command immediately causes all queued I/O to fail.
Replace the *device_ID* with the ID for your device. For example, enter

```
sudo dmsetup message 3600601607cf30e00184589a37a31d911 0 fail_if_no_path
```

To set up queuing I/O for scenarios where all paths fail:

1. Open a terminal console.

2. Open the `/etc/multipath.conf` file in a text editor.

3. Uncomment the defaults section and its ending bracket, then add the `default_features` setting, as follows:

```
defaults {
   default_features "1 queue_if_no_path"
}
```

4. After you modify the `/etc/multipath.conf` file, you must run **dracut** `-f` to re-create the `initrd` on your system, then reboot in order for the changes to take effect.

Managing I/O in Error Situations

5. When you are ready to return to failover for the device I/O, enter

```
sudo dmsetup message mapname 0 fail_if_no_path
```

Replace the *mapname* with the mapped alias name or the device ID for the device. The 0 value represents the sector and is used when sector information is not needed.
This command immediately causes all queued I/O to fail and propagates the error to the calling application.

15.14.5   Resolving Stalled I/O

If all paths fail concurrently and I/O is queued and stalled, do the following:

1. Enter the following command at a terminal console prompt:

```
sudo dmsetup message mapname 0 fail_if_no_path
```

Replace *mapname* with the correct device ID or mapped alias name for the device. The 0 value represents the sector and is used when sector information is not needed.
This command immediately causes all queued I/O to fail and propagates the error to the calling application.

2. Reactivate queuing by entering the following command:

```
sudo dmsetup message mapname 0 queue_if_no_path
```

15.14.6   Configuring Default Settings for IBM z Systems Devices

Testing of the IBM z Systems device with multipathing has shown that the dev_loss_tmo parameter should be set to 90 seconds, and the fast_io_fail_tmo parameter should be set to 5 seconds. If you are using zSeries devices, modify the /etc/multipath.conf file to specify the values as follows:

```
defaults {
```

```
        dev_loss_tmo 90
        fast_io_fail_tmo 5
}
```

The `dev_loss_tmo` parameter sets the number of seconds to wait before marking a multipath link as bad. When the path fails, any current I/O on that failed path fails. The default value varies according to the device driver being used. The valid range of values is 0 to 600 seconds. To use the driver's internal timeouts, set the value to zero (0) or to any value greater than 600.

The `fast_io_fail_tmo` parameter sets the length of time to wait before failing I/O when a link problem is detected. I/O that reaches the driver fails. If I/O is in a blocked queue, the I/O does not fail until the `dev_loss_tmo` time elapses and the queue is unblocked.

If you modify the `/etc/multipath.conf` file, the changes are not applied until you update the multipath maps, or until the `multipathd` daemon is restarted (**systemctl restart multipathd**).

15.14.7   Using Multipath with NetApp Devices

When using multipath for NetApp devices, we recommend the following settings in the `/etc/multipath.conf` file:

- Set the default values for the following parameters globally for NetApp devices:

```
max_fds max
queue_without_daemon no
```

- Set the default values for the following parameters for NetApp devices in the hardware table:

```
dev_loss_tmo infinity
fast_io_fail_tmo 5
features "3 queue_if_no_path pg_init_retries 50"
```

15.14.8   Using --noflush with Multipath Devices

The `--noflush` option should always be used when running on multipath devices.

For example, in scripts where you perform a table reload, you use the `--noflush` option on resume to ensure that any outstanding I/O is not flushed, because you need the multipath topology information.

```
load
resume --noflush
```

15.14.9   SAN Timeout Settings When the Root Device Is Multipathed

A system with root (`/`) on a multipath device might stall when all paths have failed and are removed from the system because a `dev_loss_tmo` timeout is received from the storage subsystem (such as Fibre Channel storage arrays).

If the system device is configured with multiple paths and the multipath `no_path_retry` setting is active, you should modify the storage subsystem's `dev_loss_tmo` setting accordingly to ensure that no devices are removed during an all-paths-down scenario. We strongly recommend that you set the `dev_loss_tmo` value to be equal to or higher than the `no_path_retry` setting from multipath.

The recommended setting for the storage subsystem's `dev_los_tmo` is

```
<dev_loss_tmo> = <no_path_retry> * <polling_interval>
```

where the following definitions apply for the multipath values:

- `no_path_retry` is the number of retries for multipath I/O until the path is considered to be lost, and queuing of IO is stopped.

- `polling_interval` is the time in seconds between path checks.

Each of these multipath values should be set from the `/etc/multipath.conf` configuration file. For information, see *Section 15.6, "Creating or Modifying the /etc/multipath.conf File"*.

15.15   Troubleshooting MPIO

This section describes some known issues and possible solutions for MPIO.

15.15.1   The System Exits to Emergency Shell at Boot When Multipath Is Enabled

During boot the system exits into the emergency shell with messages similar to the following:

```
[  OK  ] Listening on multipathd control socket.
         Starting Device-Mapper Multipath Device Controller...
[  OK  ] Listening on Device-mapper event daemon FIFOs.
         Starting Device-mapper event daemon...
         Expecting device dev-disk-by\x2duuid-34be48b2\x2dc21...32dd9.device...
         Expecting device dev-sda2.device...
[  OK  ] Listening on udev Kernel Socket.
[  OK  ] Listening on udev Control Socket.
         Starting udev Coldplug all Devices...
         Expecting device dev-disk-by\x2duuid-1172afe0\x2d63c...5d0a7.device...
         Expecting device dev-disk-by\x2duuid-c4a3d1de\x2d4dc...ef77d.device...
[  OK  ] Started Create list of required static device nodes ...current kernel.
         Starting Create static device nodes in /dev...
[  OK  ] Started Collect Read-Ahead Data.
[  OK  ] Started Device-mapper event daemon.
[  OK  ] Started udev Coldplug all Devices.
         Starting udev Wait for Complete Device Initialization...
[  OK  ] Started Replay Read-Ahead Data.
         Starting Load Kernel Modules...
         Starting Remount Root and Kernel File Systems...
[  OK  ] Started Create static devices
[   13.682489] floppy0: no floppy controllers found
[*     ] (1 of 4) A start job is running for dev-disk-by\x2du...(7s / 1min 30s)
[*     ] (1 of 4) A start job is running for dev-disk-by\x2du...(7s / 1min 30s)


...


Timed out waiting for device dev-disk-by\x2duuid-c4a...cfef77d.device.
[DEPEND] Dependency failed for /opt.
[DEPEND] Dependency failed for Local File Systems.
[DEPEND] Dependency failed for Postfix Mail Transport Agent.
```

```
Welcome to emergency shell
Give root password for maintenance
(or press Control-D to continue):
```

This issue is a logical consequence of the multipath integration in systemd and occurs if the root file system is not on multipath but multipath is enabled. In such a setup, multipath tries to set its paths for all devices that are not blacklisted. Since the device with the root file system is already mounted, it is inaccessible for multipath and causes it to fail.

Fix this issue by configuring multipath correctly by blacklisting the root device in `/etc/multipath.conf`:

1. Run **`multipath -v2`** in the emergency shell and identify the device for the root file system. It will result in an output similar to:

   ```
   root # multipath -v2
   Dec 18 10:10:03 | 3600508b1001030343841423043300400: ignoring map
   ```

   The string between `|` and `:` is the WWID needed for blacklisting.

2. Open `/etc/multipath.conf` and add the following:

   ```
   blacklist {
     wwid "WWWID"
   }
   ```

   Replace *WWWID* with the ID you retrieved in the previous step. For more information see *Section 15.8, "Blacklisting Non-Multipath Devices"*.

3. Exit the emergency shell and reboot the server by pressing `Ctrl`–`D`.

15.15.2 Enabling boot.multipath

Multipath must be loaded before LVM to ensure that multipath maps are built correctly. Loading multipath after LVM can result in incomplete device maps for a multipath device because LVM locks the device, and MPIO cannot create the maps properly.

If the system device is a local device that does not use MPIO and LVM, you can disable both `boot.multipath` and `boot.lvm`. After the server starts, you can manually start multipath before you start LVM, then run a **pvscan** command to recognize the LVM objects.

15.15.3   Troubleshooting MPIO Mapping for LVM Devices

Timing is important for starting the LVM process. If LVM starts before MPIO maps are done, LVM might use a fixed path for the device instead of its multipath. The device works, so you might not be aware that the device's MPIO map is incomplete until that fixed path fails. You can help prevent the problem by enabling `boot.multipath` and following the instructions in *Section 15.15.2, "Enabling boot.multipath"*.

To troubleshoot a mapping problem, you can use **dmsetup** to check that the expected number of paths are present for each multipath device. As the `root` user, enter the following at a command prompt:

```
sudo dmsetup ls --tree
```

In the following sample response, the first device has four paths. The second device is a local device with a single path. The third device has two paths. The distinction between active and passive paths is not reported through this tool.

```
tux > sudo dmsetup ls --tree
  vg910-lv00 (253:23)
     └ 360a9800064655766657346d4b6c593362 (253:10)
      |- (65:96)
      |- (8:128)
      |- (8:240)
      └ (8:16)
  vg00-lv08 (253:9)
     └ (8:3)
  system_vg-data_lv (253:1)
     └36006016088d014007e0d0d2213ecdf11 (253:0)
      ├ (8:32)
      └ (8:48)
```

An incorrect mapping typically returns too few paths and does not have a major number of 253. For example, the following shows what an incorrect mapping looks like for the third device:

```
system_vg-data_lv (8:31)
    └─ (8:32)
```

15.15.4 PRIO Settings for Individual Devices Fail After Upgrading to Multipath 0.4.9 or Later

Multipath Tools from version 0.4.9 onward uses the `prio` setting in the `defaults{}` or `devices{}` section of the `/etc/multipath.conf` file. It silently ignores the keyword `prio` when it is specified for an individual `multipath` definition in the `multipaths{}` section.

Multipath Tools 0.4.8 allowed the prio setting in the individual `multipath` definition in the `multipaths{}` section to override the `prio` settings in the `defaults{}` or `devices{}` section.

15.15.5 PRIO Settings with Arguments Fail After Upgrading to multipath-tools-0.4.9 or Later

When you upgrade from `multipath-tools-0.4.8` to `multipath-tools-0.4.9`, the `prio` settings in the `/etc/multipath.conf` file are broken for prioritizers that require an argument. In multipath-tools-0.4.9, the `prio` keyword is used to specify the prioritizer, and the `prio_args` keyword is used to specify the argument for prioritizers that require an argument. Previously, both the prioritizer and its argument were specified on the same `prio` line.

For example, in multipath-tools-0.4.8, the following line was used to specify a prioritizer and its arguments on the same line.

```
prio "weightedpath hbtl [1,3]:.:.+:.+ 260 [0,2]:.:.+:.+ 20"
```

After upgrading to multipath-tools-0.4.9 or later, the command causes an error. The message is similar to the following:

```
<Month day hh:mm:ss> | Prioritizer 'weightedpath hbtl [1,3]:.:.+:.+ 260
[0,2]:.:.+:.+ 20' not found in /lib64/multipath
```

To resolve this problem, use a text editor to modify the `prio` line in the `/etc/multipath.conf` file. Create two lines with the prioritizer specified on the `prio` line, and the prioritizer argument specified on the `prio_args` line below it:

```
prio "weightedpath"
prio_args "hbtl [1,3]:.:.+:.+ 260 [0,2]:.:.+:.+ 20"
```

Restart the `multipathd` daemon for the changes to become active by running **sudo systemctl restart multipathd**.

15.15.6 Technical Information Documents

For information about troubleshooting multipath I/O issues on SUSE Linux Enterprise Server, see the following Technical Information Documents (TIDs) in the SUSE Knowledgebase:

- *Troubleshooting SLES Multipathing (MPIO) Problems (TID 3231766)* [http://www.suse.com/support/kb/doc.php?id = 3231766]

- *DM MPIO Device Blacklisting Not Honored in multipath.conf (TID 3029706)* [http://www.suse.com/support/kb/doc.php?id = 3029706]

- *Troubleshooting SCSI (LUN) Scanning Issues (TID 3955167)* [http://www.suse.com/support/kb/doc.php?id = 3955167]

- *Using LVM on Multipath (DM MPIO) Devices* [http://www.suse.com/support/kb/doc.php?id = 7007498]

16 Managing Access Control Lists over NFSv4

There is no single standard for Access Control Lists (ACLs) in Linux beyond the simple read, write, and execute (rwx) flags for user, group, and others (ugo). One option for finer control is the *Draft POSIX ACLs*, which were never formally standardized by POSIX. Another is the NFSv4 ACLs, which were designed to be part of the NFSv4 network file system with the goal of making something that provided reasonable compatibility between POSIX systems on Linux and WIN32 systems on Microsoft Windows.

NFSv4 ACLs are not sufficient to correctly implement Draft POSIX ACLs so no attempt has been made to map ACL accesses on an NFSv4 client (such as using **setfacl**).

When using NFSv4, Draft POSIX ACLs cannot be used even in emulation and NFSv4 ACLs need to be used directly; that means while **setfacl** can work on NFSv3, it cannot work on NFSv4. To allow NFSv4 ACLs to be used on an NFSv4 file system, SUSE Linux Enterprise Server provides the nfs4-acl-tools package, which contains the following:

- **nfs4-getfacl**

- **nfs4-setfacl**

- **nfs4-editacl**

These operate in a generally similar way to **getfacl** and **setfacl** for examining and modifying NFSv4 ACLs. These commands are effective only if the file system on the NFS server provides full support for NFSv4 ACLs. Any limitation imposed by the server will affect programs running on the client in that some particular combinations of Access Control Entries (ACEs) might not be possible.

It is not supported to mount NFS volumes locally on the exporting NFS server.

Additional Information

For information, see *Introduction to NFSv4 ACLs* at http://wiki.linux-nfs.org/wiki/index.php/ACLs#Introduction_to_NFSv4_ACLs.

V Troubleshooting

17 Troubleshooting Storage Issues

This section describes how to work around known issues for devices, software RAIDs, multipath I/O, and volumes.

- *Section 1.6, "Troubleshooting File Systems"*

- *Section 6.3, "Troubleshooting Software RAIDs"*

- *Section 13.5, "Troubleshooting iSCSI"*

- *Section 15.15, "Troubleshooting MPIO"*

A Documentation Updates

This chapter lists content changes for this document.

This manual was updated on the following dates:

A.1 December 2015 (Initial Release of SUSE Linux Enterprise Server 12 SP1)

General

- *Book "Subscription Management Tool for SLES 12 SP1"* is now part of the documentation for SUSE Linux Enterprise Server.

- Add-ons provided by SUSE have been renamed to modules and extensions. The manuals have been updated to reflect this change.

- Numerous small fixes and additions to the documentation, based on technical feedback.

- The registration service has been changed from Novell Customer Center to SUSE Customer Center.

- In YaST, you will now reach *Network Settings* via the *System* group. *Network Devices* is gone (https://bugzilla.suse.com/show_bug.cgi?id=867809).

- Mentioned that subvolumes with the option `no copy on write` for `/var/lib/mariadb`, `/var/lib/pgsql`, and `/var/lib/libvirt/images` are created by default to avoid extensive fragmenting with Btrfs.

- Mentioned compression with Btrf and its implications, see *Section 1.2.1.2.1, "Mounting Compressed Btrfs File Systems"* (Fate #316463).

- Added *Section 1.6.2, "Freeing Unused Filesystem Blocks"* (https://bugzilla.suse.com/show_bug.cgi?id=951783).

Chapter 4, LVM Configuration

- Added a tip on the option `--resizefs` for the commands **lvextend**, **lvresize**, and **lvreduce** to *Section 4.8.1, "Resizing a Logical Volume with Commands"*.

Chapter 6, Software RAID Configuration

- Added *Section 6.3.1, "Recovery after Failing Disk is Back Again"* (Fate #316381).

Chapter 12, iSNS for Linux

- Updated commands to restart iSCSI service and target in *Section 12.3.2, "Adding iSCSI Nodes to a Discovery Domain"* (Fate #317929).

Chapter 15, Managing Multipath I/O for Devices

- Fixed a wrong command in *Section 15.14.2, "Scanning for New Partitioned Devices without Rebooting"* (Doc Comment #27121).

Bugfixes

- Added *Section 1.6.2, "Freeing Unused Filesystem Blocks"* (https://bugzilla.suse.com/show_bug.cgi?id=951783).

- `/var/lib/open-iscsi moved` (https://bugzilla.suse.com/show_bug.cgi?id=952469).

- KIWI build fails because of noudevsync (https://bugzilla.suse.com/show_bug.cgi?id=943298).

- VM `volume_list` description error (https://bugzilla.suse.com/show_bug.cgi?id=951321).

- Removed hint on restriction of 256 logical volumes (only applies to lvm1) (https://bugzilla.suse.com/show_bug.cgi?id=947941).

- Replaced "memory space" with "storage space" (https://bugzilla.suse.com/show_bug.cgi?id=948174).

- Added a tip on the option `--resizefs` for LVM resizing commands (https://bugzilla.suse.com/show_bug.cgi?id=947952).

- lvmetad is Enabled by Default on SLE 12 SP1 (https://bugzilla.suse.com/show_bug.cgi?id=948178).

- Corrected LVM introduction (https://bugzilla.suse.com/show_bug.cgi?id=947949).

- Removed a duplicated paragraph on thinly provisioned LVM (https://bugzilla.suse.com/show_bug.cgi?id=947484).

- `/boot` may reside on RAID 1 in *Chapter 7, Configuring Software RAID 1 for the Root Partition* (https://bugzilla.suse.com/show_bug.cgi?id=939197).

- Replaced *Login* with *Connect* in *Section 13.3.1.3, "Discovering iSCSI Targets Manually"* (https://bugzilla.suse.com/show_bug.cgi?id=939529).

- use_lvmetad, Change Does not Describe Required Target Value (https://bugzilla.suse.com/show_bug.cgi?id=939519).

A.2 February 2015 (Documentation Maintenance Update)

General

- Completely restructured the manual by introducing parts.

- Completely revised the complete guide.

- Shortened the majority of procedures.

- The `cciss` driver has been replaced with the `hpsa` driver. Changed all affected paragraphs accordingly (Fate #316683).

Chapter 1, Overview of File Systems in Linux

- Added *Section 1.2.1.2, "The Root File System Setup on SUSE Linux Enterprise Server"*.

- Added *Section 1.2.1.5, "Btrfs Quota Support for Subvolumes"* (Fate #315690).

- Added *Section 1.2.1.6, "Data Deduplication Support"* (Fate #316317).

- Added ReiserFs to the list of file systems that can be converted to Btrfs (Fate #313096).

- Added a note on the new XFS on-disk format to *Section 1.2.2.3, "Preallocation to Avoid File System Fragmentation"* (Fate #317042).

- Added *Section 1.2.5, "Ext4"*.

- Added a note about the support status of ReiserFs to *Section 1.2.6, "ReiserFS"* (Fate #313799).

Chapter 2, Resizing File Systems

- Added *Section 2.1, "Use Cases"*.

- Added *Section 2.3, "Changing the Size of a Btrfs File System"* (Fate #310777).

- Added *Section 2.4, "Changing the Size of an XFS File System"*.

Chapter 4, LVM Configuration

- Updated all parts dealing with the YaST Partitioner, because of a new design and workflow.

- Added instructions on how to list physical volumes used by logical volumes to *Section 4.5, "Resizing an Existing Volume Group"* (Fate #316074).

- Added *Section 4.8.2, "Dynamic Aggregation of LVM Metadata via* lvmetad*"* (Fate #314556).

Chapter 6, Software RAID Configuration

- Updated all parts dealing with the YaST Partitioner, because of a new design and workflow.

- Added *Section 6.2.1, "RAID Names"* (Fate #315590).

Chapter 8, Creating Software RAID 10 Devices

- Removed RAID 6 from this chapter, since setting up RAID 6 arrays is now supported by the YaST Partitioner.

- Added *Section 8.2, "Creating a Complex RAID 10"*.

- Removed all discovery domain set content, since this is no longer supported by open-isns.

- Replaced iSCSI Target with iSCSI LIO Target.

- Restructured the whole chapter.

- Removed `prio_callout` from *Section 15.10.2, "Configuring Failover Priorities"*, since it is no longer supported.

- Added *Section 15.14, "Best Practice"*.

Bugfixes

- Replace ReiserFS by Ext3 for Shrinking LV (https://bugzilla.suse.com/show_bug.cgi?id=884287).

- System Drops Into Emergency Shell After Enabling Multipath (https://bugzilla.suse.com/show_bug.cgi?id=889317/).

- There is no iSCSI Target in the Package List (https://bugzilla.suse.com/show_bug.cgi?id=905239).

A.3   October 2014 (Initial Release of SUSE Linux Enterprise Server 12)

General

- Removed all KDE documentation and references because KDE is no longer shipped.

- Removed all references to SuSEconfig, which is no longer supported (Fate #100011).

- Move from System V init to systemd (Fate #310421). Updated affected parts of the documentation.

- YaST Runlevel Editor has changed to Services Manager (Fate #312568). Updated affected parts of the documentation.

- Removed all references to ISDN support, as ISDN support has been removed (Fate #314594).

- Removed all references to the YaST DSL module as it is no longer shipped (Fate #316264).

- Removed all references to the YaST Modem module as it is no longer shipped (Fate #316264).

- Btrfs has become the default file system for the root partition (Fate #315901). Updated affected parts of the documentation.

- The **dmesg** now provides human-readable time stamps in `ctime()` -like format (Fate #316056). Updated affected parts of the documentation.

- syslog and syslog-ng have been replaced by rsyslog (Fate #316175). Updated affected parts of the documentation.

- MariaDB is now shipped as the relational database instead of MySQL (Fate #313595). Updated affected parts of the documentation.

- SUSE-related products are no longer available from http://download.novell.com but from http://download.suse.com. Adjusted links accordingly.

- Novell Customer Center has been replaced with SUSE Customer Center. Updated affected parts of the documentation.

- `/var/run` is mounted as tmpfs (Fate #303793). Updated affected parts of the documentation.

- The following architectures are no longer supported: Itanium and x86. Updated affected parts of the documentation.

- The traditional method for setting up the network with `ifconfig` has been replaced by `wicked`. Updated affected parts of the documentation.

- A lot of networking commands are deprecated and have been replaced by newer commands (usually **ip**). Updated affected parts of the documentation.

```
arp: ip neighbor
ifconfig: ip addr, ip link
iptunnel: ip tunnel
iwconfig: iw
```

```
nameif: ip link, ifrename
netstat: ss, ip route, ip -s link, ip maddr
route: ip route
```

- Numerous small fixes and additions to the documentation, based on technical feedback.

B GNU Licenses

This appendix contains the GNU Free Documentation License version 1.2.

GNU Free Documentation License

Copyright (C) 2000, 2001, 2002 Free Software Foundation, Inc. 51 Franklin St, Fifth Floor, Boston, MA 02110-1301 USA. Everyone is permitted to copy and distribute verbatim copies of this license document, but changing it is not allowed.

0. PREAMBLE

The purpose of this License is to make a manual, textbook, or other functional and useful document "free" in the sense of freedom: to assure everyone the effective freedom to copy and redistribute it, with or without modifying it, either commercially or non-commercially. Secondarily, this License preserves for the author and publisher a way to get credit for their work, while not being considered responsible for modifications made by others.

This License is a kind of "copyleft", which means that derivative works of the document must themselves be free in the same sense. It complements the GNU General Public License, which is a copyleft license designed for free software.

We have designed this License to use it for manuals for free software, because free software needs free documentation: a free program should come with manuals providing the same freedoms that the software does. But this License is not limited to software manuals; it can be used for any textual work, regardless of subject matter or whether it is published as a printed book. We recommend this License principally for works whose purpose is instruction or reference.

1. APPLICABILITY AND DEFINITIONS

This License applies to any manual or other work, in any medium, that contains a notice placed by the copyright holder saying it can be distributed under the terms of this License. Such a notice grants a world-wide, royalty-free license, unlimited in duration, to use that work under the conditions stated herein. The "Document", below, refers to any such manual or work. Any member of the public is a licensee, and is addressed as "you". You accept the license if you copy, modify or distribute the work in a way requiring permission under copyright law.

A "Modified Version" of the Document means any work containing the Document or a portion of it, either copied verbatim, or with modifications and/or translated into another language.

A "Secondary Section" is a named appendix or a front-matter section of the Document that deals exclusively with the relationship of the publishers or authors of the Document to the Document's overall subject (or to related matters) and contains nothing that could fall directly within that overall subject. (Thus, if the Document is in part a textbook of mathematics, a Secondary Section may not explain any mathematics.) The relationship could be a matter of historical connection with the subject or with related matters, or of legal, commercial, philosophical, ethical or political position regarding them.

The "Invariant Sections" are certain Secondary Sections whose titles are designated, as being those of Invariant Sections, in the notice that says that the Document is released under this License. If a section does not fit the above definition of Secondary then it is not allowed to be designated as Invariant. The Document may contain zero Invariant Sections. If the Document does not identify any Invariant Sections then there are none.

The "Cover Texts" are certain short passages of text that are listed, as Front-Cover Texts or Back-Cover Texts, in the notice that says that the Document is released under this License. A Front-Cover Text may be at most 5 words, and a Back-Cover Text may be at most 25 words.

A "Transparent" copy of the Document means a machine-readable copy, represented in a format whose specification is available to the general public, that is suitable for revising the document straightforwardly with generic text editors or (for images composed of pixels) generic paint programs or (for drawings) some widely available drawing editor, and that is suitable for input to text formatters or for automatic translation to a variety of formats suitable for input to text formatters. A copy made in an otherwise Transparent file format whose markup, or absence of markup, has been arranged to thwart or discourage subsequent modification by readers is not Transparent. An image format is not Transparent if used for any substantial amount of text. A copy that is not "Transparent" is called "Opaque".

Examples of suitable formats for Transparent copies include plain ASCII without markup, Texinfo input format, LaTeX input format, SGML or XML using a publicly available DTD, and standard-conforming simple HTML, PostScript or PDF designed for human modification. Examples of transparent image formats include PNG, XCF and JPG. Opaque formats include proprietary formats that can be read and edited only by proprietary word processors, SGML or XML for which the DTD and/or processing tools are not generally available, and the machine-generated HTML, PostScript or PDF produced by some word processors for output purposes only.

The "Title Page" means, for a printed book, the title page itself, plus such following pages as are needed to hold, legibly, the material this License requires to appear in the title page. For works in formats which do not have any title page as such, "Title Page" means the text near the most prominent appearance of the work's title, preceding the beginning of the body of the text.

A section "Entitled XYZ" means a named subunit of the Document whose title either is precisely XYZ or contains XYZ in parentheses following text that translates XYZ in another language. (Here XYZ stands for a specific section name mentioned below, such as "Acknowledgements", "Dedications", "Endorsements", or "History".) To "Preserve the Title" of such a section when you modify the Document means that it remains a section "Entitled XYZ" according to this definition.

The Document may include Warranty Disclaimers next to the notice which states that this License applies to the Document. These Warranty Disclaimers are considered to be included by reference in this License, but only as regards disclaiming warranties: any other implication that these Warranty Disclaimers may have is void and has no effect on the meaning of this License.

2. VERBATIM COPYING

You may copy and distribute the Document in any medium, either commercially or noncommercially, provided that this License, the copyright notices, and the license notice saying this License applies to the Document are reproduced in all copies, and that you add no other conditions whatsoever to those of this License. You may not use technical measures to obstruct or control the reading or further copying of the copies you make or distribute. However, you may accept compensation in exchange for copies. If you distribute a large enough number of copies you must also follow the conditions in section 3.

You may also lend copies, under the same conditions stated above, and you may publicly display copies.

3. COPYING IN QUANTITY

If you publish printed copies (or copies in media that commonly have printed covers) of the Document, numbering more than 100, and the Document's license notice requires Cover Texts, you must enclose the copies in covers that carry, clearly and legibly, all these Cover Texts: Front-Cover Texts on the front cover, and Back-Cover Texts on the back cover. Both covers must also clearly and legibly identify you as the publisher of these copies. The front cover must present the full title with all words of the title equally prominent and visible. You may add other material on the covers in addition. Copying with changes limited to the covers, as long as they preserve the title of the Document and satisfy these conditions, can be treated as verbatim copying in other respects.

If the required texts for either cover are too voluminous to fit legibly, you should put the first ones listed (as many as fit reasonably) on the actual cover, and continue the rest onto adjacent pages.

If you publish or distribute Opaque copies of the Document numbering more than 100, you must either include a machine-readable Transparent copy along with each Opaque copy, or state in or with each Opaque copy a computer-network location from which the general network-using public has access to download using public-standard network protocols a complete Transparent copy of the Document, free of added material. If you use the latter option, you must take reasonably prudent steps, when you begin distribution of Opaque copies in quantity, to ensure that this Transparent copy will remain thus accessible at the stated location until at least one year after the last time you distribute an Opaque copy (directly or through your agents or retailers) of that edition to the public.

It is requested, but not required, that you contact the authors of the Document well before redistributing any large number of copies, to give them a chance to provide you with an updated version of the Document.

4. MODIFICATIONS

You may copy and distribute a Modified Version of the Document under the conditions of sections 2 and 3 above, provided that you release the Modified Version under precisely this License, with the Modified Version filling the role of the Document, thus licensing distribution and modification of the Modified Version to whoever possesses a copy of it. In addition, you must do these things in the Modified Version:

A. Use in the Title Page (and on the covers, if any) a title distinct from that of the Document, and from those of previous versions (which should, if there were any, be listed in the History section of the Document). You may use the same title as a previous version if the original publisher of that version gives permission.

B. List on the Title Page, as authors, one or more persons or entities responsible for authorship of the modifications in the Modified Version, together with at least five of the principal authors of the Document (all of its principal authors, if it has fewer than five), unless they release you from this requirement.

C. State on the Title page the name of the publisher of the Modified Version, as the publisher.

D. Preserve all the copyright notices of the Document.

E. Add an appropriate copyright notice for your modifications adjacent to the other copyright notices.

F. Include, immediately after the copyright notices, a license notice giving the public permission to use the Modified Version under the terms of this License, in the form shown in the Addendum below.

G. Preserve in that license notice the full lists of Invariant Sections and required Cover Texts given in the Document's license notice.

H. Include an unaltered copy of this License.

I. Preserve the section Entitled "History", Preserve its Title, and add to it an item stating at least the title, year, new authors, and publisher of the Modified Version as given on the Title Page. If there is no section Entitled "History" in the Document, create one stating the title, year, authors, and publisher of the Document as given on its Title Page, then add an item describing the Modified Version as stated in the previous sentence.

J. Preserve the network location, if any, given in the Document for public access to a Transparent copy of the Document, and likewise the network locations given in the Document for previous versions it was based on. These may be placed in the "History" section. You may omit a network location for a work that was published at least four years before the Document itself, or if the original publisher of the version it refers to gives permission.

K. For any section Entitled "Acknowledgements" or "Dedications", Preserve the Title of the section, and preserve in the section all the substance and tone of each of the contributor acknowledgements and/or dedications given therein.

L. Preserve all the Invariant Sections of the Document, unaltered in their text and in their titles. Section numbers or the equivalent are not considered part of the section titles.

M. Delete any section Entitled "Endorsements". Such a section may not be included in the Modified Version.

N. Do not retitle any existing section to be Entitled "Endorsements" or to conflict in title with any Invariant Section.

O. Preserve any Warranty Disclaimers.

If the Modified Version includes new front-matter sections or appendices that qualify as Secondary Sections and contain no material copied from the Document, you may at your option designate some or all of these sections as invariant. To do this, add their titles to the list of Invariant Sections in the Modified Version's license notice. These titles must be distinct from any other section titles.

You may add a section Entitled "Endorsements", provided it contains nothing but endorsements of your Modified Version by various parties--for example, statements of peer review or that the text has been approved by an organization as the authoritative definition of a standard.

You may add a passage of up to five words as a Front-Cover Text, and a passage of up to 25 words as a Back-Cover Text, to the end of the list of Cover Texts in the Modified Version. Only one passage of Front-Cover Text and one of Back-Cover Text may be added by (or through arrangements made by) any one entity. If the Document already includes a cover text for the same cover, previously added by you or by arrangement made by the same entity you are acting on behalf of, you may not add another; but you may replace the old one, on explicit permission from the previous publisher that added the old one.

The author(s) and publisher(s) of the Document do not by this License give permission to use their names for publicity for or to assert or imply endorsement of any Modified Version.

5. COMBINING DOCUMENTS

You may combine the Document with other documents released under this License, under the terms defined in section 4 above for modified versions, provided that you include in the combination all of the Invariant Sections of all of the original documents, unmodified, and list them all as Invariant Sections of your combined work in its license notice, and that you preserve all their Warranty Disclaimers.

The combined work need only contain one copy of this License, and multiple identical Invariant Sections may be replaced with a single copy. If there are multiple Invariant Sections with the same name but different contents, make the title of each such section unique by adding at the end of it, in parentheses, the name of the original author or publisher of that section if known, or else a unique number. Make the same adjustment to the section titles in the list of Invariant Sections in the license notice of the combined work.

In the combination, you must combine any sections Entitled "History" in the various original documents, forming one section Entitled "History"; likewise combine any sections Entitled "Acknowledgements", and any sections Entitled "Dedications". You must delete all sections Entitled "Endorsements".

6. COLLECTIONS OF DOCUMENTS

You may make a collection consisting of the Document and other documents released under this License, and replace the individual copies of this License in the various documents with a single copy that is included in the collection, provided that you follow the rules of this License for verbatim copying of each of the documents in all other respects.

You may extract a single document from such a collection, and distribute it individually under this License, provided you insert a copy of this License into the extracted document, and follow this License in all other respects regarding verbatim copying of that document.

7. AGGREGATION WITH INDEPENDENT WORKS

A compilation of the Document or its derivatives with other separate and independent documents or works, in or on a volume of a storage or distribution medium, is called an "aggregate" if the copyright resulting from the compilation is not used to limit the legal rights of the compilation's users beyond what the individual works permit. When the Document is included in an aggregate, this License does not apply to the other works in the aggregate which are not themselves derivative works of the Document.

If the Cover Text requirement of section 3 is applicable to these copies of the Document, then if the Document is less than one half of the entire aggregate, the Document's Cover Texts may be placed on covers that bracket the Document within the aggregate, or the electronic equivalent of covers if the Document is in electronic form. Otherwise they must appear on printed covers that bracket the whole aggregate.

8. TRANSLATION

Translation is considered a kind of modification, so you may distribute translations of the Document under the terms of section 4. Replacing Invariant Sections with translations requires special permission from their copyright holders, but you may include translations of some or all Invariant Sections in addition to the original versions of these Invariant Sections. You may include a translation of this License, and all the license notices in the Document, and any Warranty Disclaimers, provided that you also include the original English version of this License and the original versions of those notices and disclaimers. In case of a disagreement between the translation and the original version of this License or a notice or disclaimer, the original version will prevail.

If a section in the Document is Entitled "Acknowledgements", "Dedications", or "History", the requirement (section 4) to Preserve its Title (section 1) will typically require changing the actual title.

9. TERMINATION

You may not copy, modify, sublicense, or distribute the Document except as expressly provided for under this License. Any other attempt to copy, modify, sublicense or distribute the Document is void, and will automatically terminate your rights under this License. However, parties who have received copies, or rights, from you under this License will not have their licenses terminated so long as such parties remain in full compliance.

10. FUTURE REVISIONS OF THIS LICENSE

The Free Software Foundation may publish new, revised versions of the GNU Free Documentation License from time to time. Such new versions will be similar in spirit to the present version, but may differ in detail to address new problems or concerns. See http://www.gnu.org/copyleft/.

Each version of the License is given a distinguishing version number. If the Document specifies that a particular numbered version of this License "or any later version" applies to it, you have the option of following the terms and conditions either of that specified version or of any later version that has been published (not as a draft) by the Free Software Foundation. If the Document does not specify a version number of this License, you may choose any version ever published (not as a draft) by the Free Software Foundation.

ADDENDUM: How to use this License for your documents

```
Copyright (c) YEAR YOUR NAME.

Permission is granted to copy, distribute and/or modify this document

under the terms of the GNU Free Documentation License, Version 1.2

or any later version published by the Free Software Foundation;

with no Invariant Sections, no Front-Cover Texts, and no Back-Cover

 Texts.

A copy of the license is included in the section entitled "GNU

Free Documentation License".
```

If you have Invariant Sections, Front-Cover Texts and Back-Cover Texts, replace the "with...Texts." line with this:

```
with the Invariant Sections being LIST THEIR TITLES, with the

Front-Cover Texts being LIST, and with the Back-Cover Texts being LIST.
```

If you have Invariant Sections without Cover Texts, or some other combination of the three, merge those two alternatives to suit the situation.

If your document contains nontrivial examples of program code, we recommend releasing these examples in parallel under your choice of free software license, such as the GNU General Public License, to permit their use in free software.